DATE DUE		
JAN 2 8 1986		
FEB 1 8 1986		
OCT 1 8 1988		
NOV 2 0 1990		
MAR 2 4 1992		
MAY 8 1992		
FEB 1 4 1995		
MAR 2 8 1995		
MAY 5 1995		
APR 1 1997		

ABOUT
THE AUTHORS

JOHN D. holds the M.A. and Ph.D. degrees from the New School
CARTER for Social Research (New York), and the B.D. degree
from the Conservative Baptist Theological Seminary in
Denver.

He has published a variety of articles on the integration of
psychology and theology, and serves as a contributing editor to the
Journal of Psychology and Theology. He was Scholar in Residence
at the Psychological Studies Institute, Atlanta, Georgia, during the
spring of 1976. He is a member of the American Psychological
Association, the Evangelical Theological Society, and is a past
president of the Pasadena Area Psychological Association. He is
currently Professor of Psychology and acting Dean at the Rosemead
Graduate School of Professional Psychology.

S. BRUCE holds the M.A. degree from Pepperdine University
NARRAMORE and the Ph.D. degree from the University of Ken-
tucky. He has also taken theological study at Fuller
Theological Seminary and Talbot Theological Seminary.

He was the founding Dean of the Rosemead Graduate School
of Professional Psychology and serves as a contributing editor to the
Journal of Psychology and Theology. He has lectured extensively on
the relationship of psychology and theology, including giving the
Staley Distinguished Christian Scholar Lecture Series at Covenant
Theological Seminary in 1978. He is a member of the American
Psychological Association and the Christian Association for Psychological Studies, and is a past president of the Western Association of Christians for Psychological Studies. He is currently Professor
of Psychology at the Rosemead Graduate School of Professional
Psychology.

THE
INTEGRATION
OF PSYCHOLOGY
AND
THEOLOGY

THE
INTEGRATION
OF PSYCHOLOGY
AND
THEOLOGY

An Introduction

JOHN D. CARTER
BRUCE NARRAMORE

ZONDERVAN
PUBLISHING HOUSE
OF THE ZONDERVAN CORPORATION
GRAND RAPIDS, MICHIGAN 49506

The Integration of Psychology and Theology: An Introduction
Copyright © 1979 by The Zondervan Corporation
Grand Rapids, Michigan

Library of Congress Cataloging in Publication Data
Carter, John D
    The integration of psychology and theology.
    (Rosemead psychology series)
    Bibliography: p.
    Includes index.
    1. Christianity—Psychology. I. Narramore, Bruce, joint author. II. Title.
III. Series.
BR110.C36   261.5   79-16125
ISBN 0-310-30341-9

Scripture quotations are from the Holy Bible, New International Version,
copyright © 1978 by New York International Bible Society.

Printed in the United States of America

83 84 85 86 87 88 — 10 9 8 7 6

THE ROSEMEAD PSYCHOLOGY SERIES

The Rosemead Psychology Series is a continuing series of studies written for professionals and students in the fields of psychology and theology and in related areas such as pastoral counseling. It seeks to present current thinking on the subject of the integration of psychology and the Christian faith by examining key issues and problems that grow out of the interface of psychology and theology. The data and theories of both theoretical and applied psychology are treated in this series, as well as fundamental theological concepts and issues that bear on psychological research, theory, and practice. These volumes are offered with the hope that they will stimulate further thinking and publication on the integration of psychology and the Christian faith.

Editor

BRUCE NARRAMORE
Professor of Psychology
Rosemead Graduate School
of Professional Psychology

Consulting Editors

JOHN D. CARTER
Professor of Psychology
Rosemead Graduate School
of Professional Psychology

J. ROLAND FLECK
Associate Professor of Psychology
Rosemead Graduate School
of Professional Psychology

CONTENTS

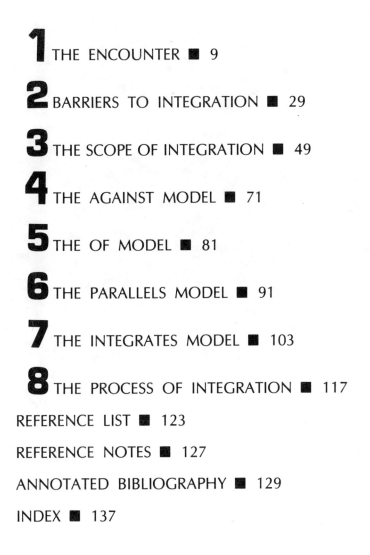

THE
ENCOUNTER

Christianity is in the throes of an encounter with psychology. On academic and popular levels alike, psychology is making inroads into areas traditionally considered the domain of Christianity. And the signs of this encounter are everywhere about us.

Religious bookstores are filled with volumes on psychology. A Christian periodical is incomplete without an article on some aspect of personal or family adjustment. And nearly every theological seminary offers courses in areas such as counseling, psychology, and mental health.

Psychologists are lecturing at Bible conferences. The "family-life week," with psychologically oriented speakers and seminar leaders, is fast replacing the church's revival meetings, evangelistic services, and prophetic conferences. And relational theology (Petersen and Broad, 1977) is influencing both our theological institutions and the person in the pew.

Increasingly, our society is looking to psychology to shed new light on the problems of human existence. Questions concerning the nature of the human being and psychological health and happiness are being directed increasingly to the psychological community. In fact, in many quarters the whole process of "curing sick souls" is rapidly moving from the church to the doorsteps of psychologists and other mental health professionals. The data, theories, and methods of psychology impinge so directly on the domain of theology and Christianity that it is impossible for the church to remain neutral in the face of the rising popularity of psychology. With the possible exception of the theory of evolution in biology, psychology has already had a greater impact on the church than any other scientific discipline.

The encounter between psychology and Christianity is not one sided. A resurgent interest in the study of religion by psychologists is also under way. This interest, first evident during the early decades of this century (James, 1901/1952; Starbuck, 1901), appears to have virtually died out during the 1930s, 1940s, and early 1950s as psychologists became preoccupied with making psychology "scientific," in the narrowest sense of the term. Interest was rekindled at the 1959 American Psychological Association (APA) convention symposium entitled "The Role of the Concept of Sin in Psychotherapy." This renewed interest in psychology and religion accounts for the APA's recent decision to create Division 36—"Psychologists Interested in Religious Issues."

O. Hobart Mowrer, a past president of the APA, reflects this current interest. In his book *The Crisis in Psychiatry and Religion* (1961) he states:

> Religion is, of course, deeply concerned with man as person and personality; and in their shifting perception of man-as-body to man-as-person, psychology and psychiatry find themselves looking again, with renewed interest and respect, at religious precept and practice. Whatever may be the incompatability of religion and these secular disciplines in the metaphysical realm, here, in the study of personality in its social and ethical dimensions, is a natural and favorable meeting place. (p. 2)

An increasing number of psychologists, psychiatrists, and mental health professionals are pursuing the study of personality within a Christian frame of reference. One of the most significant evidences of this ongoing concern is the Christian Association for Psychological Studies, which has several hundred members who are committed to the interdisciplinary study of psychology.

THE RESPONSE　Christians have reacted in various ways to
TO PSYCHOLOGY　the rise of modern psychology. Some have
　　　　　　　　welcomed it with outstretched arms. For them, the insights of psychology are a great ally for the church as it carries out its mission in the world. Others reject psychology out of hand. They see in it an implicit threat to the church and to the authority of Scripture.

Most Christians have mixed emotions about the development of psychology. On the one hand, they see much potential in a scientific study of the human being. They know that objective data and well-constructed theories will expand our understanding of God's most complex creation. And they believe that the insights of psychology can help the church to minister more effectively to the total needs of humanity.

But, on the other hand, the rapid growth of psychology as a science and its related professions may also be viewed as an encroachment on the ministry of the church. Reaching almost faddish proportions, allegiance to psychology is drawing many away from the church. Psychology, equipped with its own brand of secular priests, is offering a form of psychological "salvation" to society. Whether rooted in the research of experimental psychologists, the ideas of psychological theorists, or the counseling skills of psychotherapists, the salvation offered here is not some future "pie in the sky." It is the desire to understand the dilemma of modern society and to offer help for more successful personal living, both of which strike a responsive chord in an age of tension and anxiety.

Many individual Christians look to psychology for new insights that will relieve personal discomfort or despair. They hope that psychology will provide answers to problems not specifically addressed in Christianity. At the same time, however, they may experience guilt at turning outside the church for help. They may even have been told that their problems are entirely spiritual and that what they really need is more faith, more Bible study, more prayer, or a deeper commitment, but certainly not psychotherapy.

Pastors and other full-time Christian workers are caught up in a similar impasse. Encountering deep emotional problems in those who come to them for counsel, they seek deeper understanding of the human personality and better principles for counseling. They know that stereotyped spiritual answers are inadequate. Yet they believe that the Bible contains the answer to the dilemma of humanity. If they look to psychology, are they tacitly admitting that the Bible is inadequate? The fear that they are being disloyal to God and to His Word stirs anxiety in many of these Christian workers.

Christian psychologists and those in related professions also face a similar problem. They believe that their discipline contains a great body of truth and they seek to apply this truth within the framework of the Christian faith. But they see many barriers. They face some clear-cut differences of opinion with their secular colleagues, and sometimes even their Christian brothers resist any attempt to relate psychological principles to the Christian life.

There are many others besides the pastor and the psychologist who are caught up in the encounter between psychology and Christianity. The theologian, the physician, and the student of psychology and theology are all concerned about the welfare of humanity, and through the practice of their discipline each hopes to better life on earth while at the same time carrying out their Christian commitment and responsibility. In order to do this they must decide what value they will place on the integration of psychology and theology. They also must decide how they are going to respond to the challenges of psychology.

At this point a word needs to be said about perspective and purpose. This volume deals with the integration of psychology and theology, and the reader has no doubt already concluded that the text will utilize material from both psychology and theology. This is entirely correct. We *assume* that both psychology and theology offer a great deal toward an understanding of the human race. Consequently, no effort has been made to establish the validity of either psychological methods or biblical revelation.

The non-Christian reader who is looking for an explanation (see Stott [1971]) or a defense (see Carnell [1948] and Ramm [1954]) of the Christian faith, a very worthwhile and essential prerequisite for this study, will not find it here. This volume is an attempt to integrate biblical and psychological concepts, not establish or defend them. Similarly, the Christian looking for a justification or defense of psychology (see Collins [1977] and Jeeves [1976]) will not find it in these pages. This volume assumes a basic commitment or openness to the data of psychology.

THE POSSIBILITY OF INTEGRATION During the last decade Christian behavioral scientists have increasingly used the word *integration* to refer to the interaction between, or "interface" of, their given discipline and the discipline of theology. This practice is especially widespread in psychology. One scholarly journal[1] has described itself as "An Evangelical Forum for the Integration of Psychology and Theology," and at least two accredited doctoral-degree programs in psychology require students to take a series of "integration seminars" designed to relate Scripture and psychology.[2] Most of these efforts are based on one essential philosophical underpinning—the belief that all truth is God's truth, wherever it is found. This proposition is frequently referred to as "the unity of truth."

The Unity of Truth

Christianity affirms that God is the Creator of all things and that this establishes a basic unity of all truth, whether found in scriptural revelation or scientific experimentation (Gaebelein, 1968; Holmes, 1977). Given this unity of truth, it is possible to integrate truth arrived at from different sources and with different methodologies. Unfortunately, while the unity of truth has been affirmed since the time of the early Christian church, this focus has been periodically

---

[1]*The Journal of Psychology and Theology,* 13800 Biola Avenue, La Mirada, California.

[2]Fuller School of Psychology in Pasadena, California, and Rosemead Graduate School of Professional Psychology in La Mirada, California.

lost by the church and has been at times almost entirely ignored by society at large.

Speaking of the church's failure to participate in meaningful integrative activities, Gaebelein (1968) writes:

> We have been too prone to set up a false dichotomy in our think-ing and thus in our education. We have rightly enthroned the Word of God as the ultimate criterion of truth; we have rightly given pre-eminence to the Lord Jesus Christ as the incarnation of the God of all truth. But at the same time, we have fallen into the error of failing to see as clearly as we should that there are areas of truth not fully explicated in Scripture and that these, too, are a part of God's truth. Thus we have made the misleading distinction between sacred and secular, forgetting that, as Cervantes said in one of those flashes of wisdom that punctuate the strange doings of Don Quixote, "Where the truth is, in so far as it is truth, there God is." (p. 21)

This book and the Rosemead Psychology Series of which it is a part are written with a fundamental commitment to this concept of the unity of truth. If all truth is God's truth, there is a basic unity between all disciplines. This unity is the basis for all attempts at integrating one's Christian faith with academic and professional pursuits.

Some have suggested that an integration of psychology and theology is either impossible, unnecessary, or both. They argue that the Bible and psychology are potentially competing truth systems, that their sources of knowledge are different, and that the issues they address are not the same. Sutherland and Poelstra (Note 5), for example, state:

> We are often asked if we are "Christian psychologists" and find it difficult to answer since we don't know what the question implies. We are Christians who are psychologists but at the present time there is no acceptable Christian psychology that is markedly different from non-Christian psychology. It is difficult to imply that we function in a manner that is fundamentally distinct from our non-Christian colleagues. Is there a distinct Christian dentistry, or surgery, or history or grammar? Certainly in some aspects we will be different than some of our non-Christian colleagues. But as yet there is not an acceptable theory, mode of research or treatment methodology that is distinctly Christian. The Bible and Psychology

are separate, distinct fields and whatever overlap exists is not sufficient to justify forced integration. It merely reduces the significance and influence of one or both fields. A person who is both Christian and psychologist functions as a whole person but that is no imperative for formal integration any more than in the fields of dentistry, surgery, law or auto mechanics. Our imperative is to be the best psychologists we possibly can be, not to formally integrate our two fields.

Sutherland and Poelstra have issued a warning against forced, superficial, or artificial integration, and this warning is well taken. Christian psychologists, especially those writing for a popular audience, have tended to take a theory proposed by a secular psychologist, include a few passages of Scripture, and pass it off as Christian. And we would also agree that as yet there is no distinctly Christian theory or model or research. But what of the claim that there is no imperative for a formal integration of psychology and theology, just as there is no need to integrate theology with dentistry, surgery, law, or auto mechanics?

While we would agree that there are competent non-Christian surgeons, dentists, lawyers, auto mechanics, and psychologists and incompetent Christian surgeons, dentists, lawyers, auto mechanics, and psychologists, are there not some inherent differences between, for example, psychology and auto mechanics that preclude integration in one of these fields but make it imperative in the other?

Both the Bible and psychology have a great deal of subject matter in common. Both study the attitudes and behavior of the human race. In this sense, they are both anthropologies. And while God has not chosen to reveal truths of auto mechanics or dentistry through Scripture, He certainly has revealed a vast amount of truth about the nature and functioning of the human personality.

A Christian Imperative

While acknowledging that a forced or artificial integration runs the risk of violating the truths of divine revelation or the facts and principles of psychology, we cannot accept a view that minimizes the possibility or the necessity of integrating our psychological understanding of persons with our understanding of the revealed truths of

Scripture. If God is the author of all truth, we need not be afraid to examine what might appear to be competing truth claims. If God is the author of all truth, we are not dealing with ultimately different sources of truth. And if issues such as personal adjustment, motivation, determinism, and the handling of negative emotions are not common to both psychology and theology, then we have in view either a truncated gospel or a very narrow psychology.

Whether we label the relating of the Bible and psychology as "integration" or as "interface" of psychology and theology or the "relationship" of faith and learning is not our main concern. What is important is the concept of wrestling with the relationship between the findings of psychology and the revelation of the Bible. The authors of the Rosemead Psychology Series believe that there is a great deal to be gained from a continuing dialogue between psychology and theology. We believe there is a biblical imperative for every Christian who works with people—be it from the pulpit or in the classroom, laboratory, or counseling office—to come to grips with an understanding of the human being that is as comprehensive as possible.

This imperative is grounded in the fact that we are created in God's image and is further developed in Genesis 1:28 in God's charge to humanity to multiply, replenish the earth, and have dominion over it. As divine image-bearers, we have both the privilege and the responsibility to expand our understanding of God's created order and to increase our dominion over it. Eric Sauer (1962) writes concerning this passage in Genesis:

> These words plainly declare the vocation of the human race to rule. They also call him to progressive growth in culture. Far from being something in conflict with God, cultural achievements are an essential attribute of the nobility of man as he possessed it in Paradise. Inventions and discoveries, the sciences and the arts, refinement and enabling, in short, the advance of the human mind, are throughout the will of God. (p. 81)

In this task of exercising dominion over the rest of creation, the church in every age has encountered new problems and gained new understanding. While we believe that scriptural revelation is complete and final, our understanding of theology is continually developing. For example, it was at the Council of Nicea (A.D. 325) that the doctrine of the Trinity was formulated; and at the Council of Chalcedon (A.D. 451) the doctrine of Christ's full humanity and full deity was clearly articulated. The focus of the Reformation was the doctrine of salvation (soteriology), which was thoroughly debated and formulated according to the now orthodox view of salvation by grace. And during the last one hundred years detailed study has been given to the sequence of prophetic events as outlined in the Book of Revelation and other prophetic Scriptures. But only recently, in the wake of the drastic deterioration of the family unit and the mass of conflicting "solutions" to this problem, have Christians begun to give attention to developing a comprehensive theology of the family (Gangel, 1977; B. Narramore, 1978).

The Problem of the Human Being

It is our belief that the phenomenal growth of interest in psychology is bringing into focus a need to refine and clarify certain areas of evangelical theology—especially those dealing with the nature of the human being. While we might wish that our theological insights would precede society's attention to an issue, historically this is often not the case. Instead, issues surfacing from the struggles of people trying to master their world, themselves, or their relationships have tended to stimulate Christians to search the Scriptures in a new and deeper way to see what light it sheds on the concern at hand.

We realize that to many the idea that the study of psychology has anything significant to offer to Christianity is a highly debatable issue. In many ways psychology itself is in disarray. Behaviorists are in conflict with humanists. Clinicians are in conflict with academicians. And the politics in psychological circles rivals that on Capitol Hill. Add to this the disappointing results of the many kinds of therapy, both secular and Christian, and it seems entirely valid to ask what, if anything, psychology has to contribute to Christianity.

However, the many problems and limitations of psychology must not blind us to the value of an ongoing study of human behavior. Who would deny, for example, that humanistic psychology's current emphasis on self-esteem and self-acceptance is not forcing the church to clarify the implications and meaning of concepts such as depravity, humility, pride, and self-love in the light of the need for a sense of dignity and worth? And who would deny that the interpersonal focus of social psychology and group psychology has not made a deep impact on the church's understanding of "community" and "body life"? Without ignoring the possibilities for misunderstanding and abuse in these areas, we must admit that psychology is helping the church by forcing it to speak to current issues.

For centuries theologians have spoken only tangentially to these issues or at least in ways that no longer speak clearly to the modern mind. If we are to keep theological formulations relevant to the culture in which we live, we must address the issues raised by the students of humanity within our culture. Berkhouwer (1962) writes: "Today, more than at any time, the question, 'What is man?' is at the center of theological and philosophical concern." (p. 9)

When viewed in the light of theology's continuing need for refinement, restatement, and contemporary application, we can see why it is so essential to pursue an integration of psychology and theology. The church has a great deal at stake in its understanding of the human being. For too long we have looked at the task of integrating the findings of psychology and Scripture as an intriguing option or perhaps a desirable possibility for those called to the study of psychology. We have said, "Yes, psychologists need to study the Scriptures to gain deeper insights into human nature." Or, "They need to study Scripture to deal with the spiritual needs of people." Or, "They need to study the Scriptures to avoid heretical teachings."

These statements are true as far as they go, but they miss the fact that the Christian's study of human beings, like the study of every facet of creation, is not an option but an imperative. It is part of our God-ordained task of exercising dominion over the earth and of relating the gospel to humanity. Because of this, the study of the relationship of the Word of God to the findings of psychology should not be restricted to psychologists. Theologians, pastors, and

Christian educators, as well as students of psychology, have much to gain from a careful study of the relationships between scriptural revelation and psychological fact and theory.

In some instances the data of psychology fit well with our current theological understanding. In other cases they raise questions that theology has yet to face. And sometimes they present a direct challenge to our theological affirmations. But in every case, the church has a responsibility to respond to the claims of psychology by restudying, clarifying, reaffirming, enlarging, or correcting its understanding.

Tangible Results

The results of such study by the church should not be purely theoretical. The quality of preaching and teaching in the church is closely tied to our understanding of theology in general and the nature of the human being in particular. Systems of Christian education rest ultimately on certain presuppositions regarding the nature of persons and the nature of reality. And Christian approaches to child rearing, husband-wife relationships, and the nature of family government flow logically out of our view of human nature. But just as pastors, theologians, and students of theology must respond to the data, insights, and theories of psychology, so too Christian psychologists, psychiatrists, and mental health workers must be willing to approach the study of their disciplines from the framework of biblical revelation.

From fundamental issues in epistemology (the nature of truth) and anthropology (human nature) to pragmatic details such as counseling techniques, every psychological theory makes assumptions that relate to biblical revelation. To fail to evaluate critically a theory of personality or a theory of counseling by its congruency with the biblical revelation on human nature and sin, for example, is to throw away the Christian's most useful resource for a complete and accurate understanding of the primary subject matter of psychology. People, being created in God's image, are not simply another link in the chain of evolution. According to Scripture, humans are more than just material. They are free and morally responsible beings (in spite of the fact that psychology has demonstrated how we can influence many aspects of human behavior). And people are not ultimately fulfilled apart from their Creator.

In almost every area of psychology, Scripture has much to say that can influence our understanding of psychological research, theory, and practice. This is what we mean by the term *integration*. Psychology is raising questions and providing data that bear on our theological understanding of the human being, and theology expresses divinely revealed truths that speak to psychology's developing view of humanity. In chapter 2 we will examine some of the barriers to the development of a truly Christian psychology. In chapter 3 we will look at the extent of this overlapping interest. And in chapters 4 through 7 we will attempt to outline four general models that have been used in relating the Bible and psychology. This will lead us to what we believe is the most productive way of approaching the task of relating the data, insights, and theories of psychology to the revealed truths of the Bible.

CONFLICTS: REAL AND IMAGINARY One reason many Christians hesitate to accept the methods and findings of psychology is because they assume that there are inherent conflicts between psychology and Christianity. Similarly, many non-Christian psychologists have steered clear of religious phenomena and concepts because of the supposed superiority of the scientific method and the fear of contaminating their endeavors with the "subjectivity" of religion. While there certainly are areas of conflict between psychological theorizing and theological interpretations, the nature and extent of these conflicts has frequently been misunderstood and exaggerated. This has led to what appears to be an adversary relationship between psychology and Christianity, and this works against the process of integration.

Early in our study we need to make clear where the potential conflicts lie and what the nature of these conflicts is. The history of Christianity is filled with incidents in which great furor was generated over what was considered to be a conflict between theology and science. Sometimes theological affirmations have been vindicated as once-popular scientific conceptions have taken their place with other outdated or unproven "facts" or theories. On other occasions, time has proven that our theology was in error and the findings of science have stood firm.

A good case in point was the church's adamant rejection of Copernicus's theory that the earth rotates on its axis daily and that it and other planets orbit the sun. At that time the suggestion that earth was not the center of the universe was outright heresy. In 1615 Galileo was called before the Inquisition at Rome because he championed the Copernican theory. White (1898) reports the comments of the Inquisition:

> The first proposition, that the sun is the center and does not revolve around the earth, is foolish, absurd, false in theology, and heretical because expressly contrary to Holy Scripture; the second proposition, that the earth is not the center but revolves about the sun, is absurd, false in philosophy, and from a theological point of view at least, opposed to the true faith. (p. 137)

Theologians of Galileo's day believed that the idea of the human race living on one planet within a universe of heavenly bodies robbed humanity of its uniqueness and significance. Gradually, however, the Copernican view gained acceptance until it is now an accepted scientific fact. In the process the church had to alter its theology. Modern theologians now reject the idea of the earth as the center of the universe somehow ensuring the centrality of the human race. Instead, they affirm that the Bible has never tied our significance in God's redemptive plan to considerations of space or time. Pointing to the fact that even Old Testament writers spoke of the brevity of life and humanity's relative physical insignificance, they affirm that our glory is found in the fact that we are in the image of God and that we need not abandon the theological centrality of the earth as the location God selected to carry out His redemptive program with the human race.

Facts and Theories

The history of interaction between theology and the sciences suggests that both disciplines have abundant reason to approach seeming conflicts with great humility. The paths of both science and theology are strewn with the debris of long-since rejected or disproven "truth." Apparently both theologians and scientists are too frequently in search of conflicts and divisions in order to prove the superiority of their respective disciplines. Some psychologists, harboring deep reservations or resentments toward the Christian faith, seem bent on utilizing the data and theory of psychology to "disprove" religion. And many equally defensive Bible teachers seem to have a need to set the teachings of biblical revelation over and against the findings and theories of psychology.

In chapter 2 we will analyze some of the reasons for this phenomenon. For the present, however, we simply want to bring one unifying concept into focus—the basic distinction in psychology between psychological fact and psychological theory and in theology between biblical revelation and biblical interpretations. Table 1 summarizes the effect of making these distinctions.

TABLE 1—FACT AND INTERPRETATION IN PSYCHOLOGY AND THEOLOGY

	DATA OF THEOLOGY (SCRIPTURE)	INTERPRETATIONS OF THEOLOGY
DATA (FACTS) OF PSYCHOLOGY	No Conflict	Possible Conflict
THEORIES OF PSYCHOLOGY	Possible Conflict	Possible Conflict

If we believe that God is the source of all truth, we assume that there is no inherent conflict between the *facts* of psychology and the *data* of Scripture. All conflicts between theology and psychology must, therefore, be conflicts between either the *facts* of Scripture and the *theories* of psychology, the *facts* of psychology and our (mis)*interpretation* of Scripture, or between the *theories* of psychology and our (mis)*interpretations* of Scripture. Malcolm Jeeves (1976) put it well:

> As a Christian, it is my belief that, ultimately, truth is one and that what God has chosen to give to man down the ages through his special messengers will not ultimately conflict with what he has encouraged us to discover as we exercise his gifts of mind and hand in exploring the created order, including, of course, man himself, his experience and his behaviour. That is not to say that there will not be a steady stream of apparent conflicts, between what, at any time, we believe to be the case from psychological research, and what we have hitherto understood the Bible to be saying. As we shall see, such conflicts will arise at times because our psychological knowledge is partial or inaccurate, and at times because we have wrongly interpreted Scripture. Either way, unreal conflicts are readily generated. (p. 18)

Increasingly we are seeing greater interaction among disciplines. Researchers, academicians, and applied professionals are all seeing the need for a more comprehensive understanding of ourselves and our world than can be gained by the narrow study of one discipline in isolation from others. In this process conflicts inevitably surface, but they are either gradually resolved or temporarily viewed as paradoxes or dilemmas.

When we come to an apparent conflict between theology and science, however, we encounter another problem. There is a tendency on the part of some to see as sacred and inspired not only the subject matter of theology (i.e., the Bible) but also the entire discipline of theology itself. This assumption places theologizing on a level by itself and works against open interdisciplinary interaction. Charles Kraft (1977) writes:

> Can the understandings of evangelical theologies be regarded as absolute and timeless just because they are understandings of a revelation from the absolute God? Or are theological interpretations to be treated as man-made, like the interpretations of any other man-made discipline?
>
> Certainly we must recognize the man-madeness and fallibility of every academic discipline. There is no essential superiority of "The Queen of the Sciences" [theology] over any other discipline, even though we may contend that the scriptural data that theologians work with is more sacred than the data ordinarily treated by other disciplines. But, as informed theologians know, the assumption of sacredness is an assumption about the data, not in the perspective from which [such] data are analyzed. (p. 170)

Theology is not the only discipline that has imputed a certain "sacredness" to its methods, presuppositions, activities, and conclusions. Scientists frequently treat their theories more as proven facts than working assumptions. In textbooks and popularized materials, for example, most scientists speak of evolution as a conclusive fact rather than a working hypothesis. And although many firmly believe there is sufficient data to justify such a conclusion, most would admit that, more properly speaking, evolution is still a theory. If we are going to have an effective integration of the revealed truths of Scripture and the findings of psychology, we must continually keep in mind the distinctions between psychological fact and psychological theory and between biblical fact and biblical interpretation.

Two brief examples of apparent conflicts between psychology and Scripture will illustrate this truth. For years large portions of the evangelical church have been influenced by the Keswick Movement. This movement, in espousing a "deeper" Christian life, has frequently taught a morbid form of self-denial and debasement that can stir up neurotic feelings of worthlessness and self-contempt in people prone to guilt and self-devaluation. One Christian author (Hession, 1950) wrote:

> Those who have been in tropical lands tell us that there is a big difference between a snake and a worm, when you attempt to strike at them. The snake rears itself up and hisses and tries to strike back—a true picture of self. But a worm offers no resistance; it allows you to do what you like with it, kick it or squash it under your heel—a picture of true brokenness. Jesus was willing to become just that for us—a worm and no man. And he did so, because that is what he saw us to be, worms having forfeited all rights by our sin, except to deserve hell. And he now calls us to take our rigthful place as worms for him and with him. (p. 15)

Responding to such misrepresentation of biblical Christianity, many psychologists have attacked the Christian faith for promoting psychologically unhealthy attitudes and for being in conflict with accepted principles of psychological health. Ellis (Note 5), for example, states that religion consequently is self debasement and self abnegation as, of course, virtually all the saints and mystics have clearly stated that it is. In the final analysis, then, religion is neurosis. This is why I remarked at a symposium on sin and psychotherapy held by the American Psychological Association a few years ago that from a mental health standpoint, Voltaire's famous dictum should be reversed, for if there were a God it would be necessary to uninvent him.

In this conflict between one view of Christianity and one psychological viewpoint we have a rather typical example of mutual misunderstanding. Although some Christians do interpret the Christian concepts of humility and sacrifice in a self-debasing manner, most theologians would agree that this is a serious distortion of scriptural teaching. Similarly, many respected psychologists (Allport, 1950; Fromm, 1950) object to Ellis's diagnosis of religion as neurosis. The apparent conflict dissolves when we take another look at biblical teachings, which in fact do not propound a neurotic self-abasement, and at psychological research, which does not support the implication of Ellis's theory.

Freud's (1913/1953; 1927/1961) assumptions about religion provide another good example of the confusion of fact and theory. In transferring his theory of the psychosexual development of the individual to his study of culture, he concluded that the idea of God is simply a myth created to cope with primitive people's anxiety in the face of natural disasters and the child's ambivalent feelings (love and hate) toward the same-sexed parent. He (1927/1961) wrote:

> We know that a human child cannot successfully complete its development to the civilized stage without passing through a phase of neurosis, sometimes of greater and sometimes of less distinctness. . . . In just the same way, one might assume, humanity as a whole, in its development through the ages, fell into states analogous to the neuroses, and for the same reasons—namely because in the times of ignorance and intellectual weakness the instinctual renunciations indispensable for man's communal existence had only been achieved by it by means of purely affective forces. The precipitates of these processes resembling repression which took place in prehistoric times still remained attached to civilization for long periods. Religion would thus be the universal obsessional neurosis of children, it arose out of the Oedipus

complex, out of the relation to the father. If this view is right, it is to be supposed that a turning-away from religion is bound to occur with the fatal inevitability of a process of growth, and that we find ourselves, at this very juncture, in the middle of that phase of development. (pp. 42-43)

Some people would hold that with this analysis Freud "disproved" religion or at least "explained God away." But as soon as Freud began speaking about the existence or nonexistence of God, he left psychology and entered the domain of philosophy and religion. Even if it could be demonstrated that people's concept of God arises from the intimate relationships with their parents, this would not justify the conclusion that God does not exist. A psychological fact is just that. It is not and can never be an ontological statement about the existence of God. If God so willed, He could have chosen to plant the rudimentary concept of Himself in the mind of every person through this very process.

Types of Understanding

This fact leads us to another basic understanding regarding the interface of theology and psychology. On many occasions when theology and psychology at first glance appear to be in conflict, we may be dealing with different levels or types of understanding or interpretation. For example, a psychological explanation of the nature and development of a religious experience (be it belief in God, conversion, etc.) does not necessarily exhaust the full meaning of the event. There may at the same time be a sociological, physiological, or theological understanding of that same phenomenon. Even if we could explain the process of religious conversion from a psychological viewpoint, we would not have an exhaustive understanding of the process. There is still the meaning of that experience in relationship to God and all of the accompanying spiritual dimensions that are not included in a psychological understanding.

The difference between a theological and a scientific understanding of death provides another example of different levels or foci of understanding. From the standpoint of medical science, we may speak of death as cessation of heartbeat or the absence of brain-wave activity. But from a theological standpoint death is the rending asunder of the essential elements of personal existence (2 Cor. 5:14). Similarly, when we speak of the *scientific* cause of death, we may refer to cancer, cardiac arrest, or cerebral hemorrhaging. These are accurate scientific explanations. But the theologian would also look at death as "the wages of sin." Because all humans are descendants of Adam and members of a sinful human race, and because the wages of sin is death, all die. This explanation is not in conflict with the scientific explanation of death. It is simply addressing another aspect or level of experience of death.

The point of these brief illustrations is this: Psychologists and theologians are frequently studying different aspects of the same phenomena or studying the same phenomenon from different perspectives. Before we hasten to find another conflict between psychology and Scripture, we need to ask ourselves first of all whether we are dealing with psychological theory, psychological fact, biblical interpretation, or biblical fact. If we conclude we are dealing with both psychological and biblical fact, we must ask whether the seeming conflict is generated by different levels or foci of study and whether both facts may not be true simultaneously since they are dealing with different types of data or levels of explanation.

Only when we have arrived at this point and still have a conflict can we say that we truly have a conflict between the facts of biblical revelation and the facts of psychology. Our position is that there is a unity of truth and such conflicts do not in fact exist. We hold that all conflicts between theology and psychology are conflicts between theory and interpretation of the facts rather than between the facts themselves.

BARRIERS
TO INTEGRATION

We have looked at the re- **2** surgence of interest in the
relationship of psychology and Christianity. Yet in spite
of a number of publications and many serious efforts, it
seems that the process of integration has only just begun. Collins
(1975) categorized the evangelical contributors to the interface of
Christianity and psychology as they relate to counseling into four
major groups that he labeled respectively as (1) pastoral counselors
(e.g., Jay Adams, 1970; Maurice Wagner, 1974); (2) Christian professionals (Don Tweedie, 1961; James Dobson, 1970; Quentin
Hyder, 1971); (3) theoretician-researchers (Paul Meehl, 1958); and
(4) the evangelical popularizers (Bill Gothard, n.d.; Tim LaHaye,
1971; Howard Hendricks, 1973; Norman Wright, 1974).

Although varying greatly in both their biblical positions and
their psychological and theological sophistication, all of these authors have played a part in bringing psychology to the attention of
the church. Many Christians, however, continue to reject the
findings of psychology. A recent statement by a popular Christian
author (Billheimer, 1977) demonstrates the suspicion and distrust

with which psychology continues to be viewed in many Christian quarters:

> Except where there is organic difficulty, the root of all conflicts in the home is not mental, but spiritual. Psychology and psychiatry are usually totally irrelevant. A spiritual problem always has a spiritual cause and requires a spiritual solution. . . . Many spiritually discerning persons are quite convinced that psychiatry is Satan's substitute for the Biblical remedy for disturbed relations. (p. 89)

Even those more inclined toward the process of integration acknowledge that we still have far to go. In fact, nearly all past efforts at the integration of psychology and theology suffer from one or more of the following deficiencies:

1. They tend to be piecemeal or based on proof-texted approaches to the problem of integration and, consequently, lack comprehensiveness.
2. They are lacking in either psychological or theological sophistication or both.
3. They attempt to press the data of Scripture onto psychology, or vice versa, in a way that is inappropriate and does not do justice to both disciplines.
4. They lack a well-defined view of the nature of the human being.
5. They lack clearly defined theological and philosophical underpinnings.
6. They lack objective scientific data.
7. They lack a well-thought-out theory of personality.
8. They lack a theory of counseling that issues out of a comprehensive view of the human being and maladjustment.

These weaknesses have resulted in a dearth of writings that are biblically consistent, psychologically "accurate," and meaningfully integrated at both the conceptual and practical levels. Until these weaknesses are overcome, it will be impossible to have a systematic and comprehensive Christian view of psychology. And it will be impossible to integrate the data of psychology and Scripture in a way that significantly benefits both disciplines.

Even at this, considering the variety of theological viewpoints within orthodox Christianity and the variety of viewpoints in psychology, it is inconceivable that we will ever have one universally agreed upon "Christian theory of psychology." Instead, we should expect several well thought-out views of the human being in accordance with biblical truth and current psychological knowledge. We should expect a continued refinement of our theological thinking regarding human nature. And we should expect to see some careful evaluations and modifications of current psychological thinking in the light of biblical revelation.

But let's back up a bit. Why is it that centuries after the Reformation and one hundred years after the founding of modern psychology the Christian church is just now beginning to grapple seriously with the discipline of psychology? Why is it that we have not gathered any significant bank of psychological data? Why have we failed to examine carefully the underlying philosophical presuppositions of secular psychology and suggest some biblical alternatives? Why have we not developed either a definitive Christian theory of personality or a general theory of behavior? In fact, why is it that in many corners of the evangelical church there remains considerable suspicion and distrust of psychological theory and data? And to look at the other side of the coin, why do many secular psychologists have serious quarrels with religion in general and evangelical Christianity in particular? Why is it that such mutual fear and skepticism exist?

Paul Barkman (1965) gives a humorous description of the mutual anxieties of psychologists and theologians when in each other's presence.

> Rather typically, if a psychologist (of psychoanalytic orientation) were to listen to a theologian (of Calvinistic orientation) discuss theology, the psychologist might be quite puzzled to find himself described as "an unregenerate soul who resists the Holy Spirit with worldly wisdom because of a depraved nature and an impenitent spirit." (Unless, of course, the psychologist were a minister's son—which many of these are.) To this he might reply that the theologian has "a paranoiac personality trait disturbance with an unresolved oedipal complex, who is engaging in projec-

tion of repressed hostility toward a castrating father figure." The theologian might return home proud of his testimony, puzzled and a little shaken, and say to his wife, "Today I met a psychoanalyst!" The psychologist might well go home to his wife proud of his educative function, somewhat anxious and perplexed, and using his wife as a therapist say, "Today I met a preacher!" (pp. 9-10)

Although misunderstandings between psychologists and theologians go far beyond the bounds of either Calvinism or psychoanalysis, Barkman's illustration does highlight the problems of language and perspective facing professionals from such divergent disciplines as psychology and theology. In this chapter we would like to go further and suggest several other reasons for our past failure to establish a distinctively Christian psychology and to allow the findings of psychology to constructively impact the church. The first few reasons arise out of the twentieth-century historical development in the Christian church, especially the effect of the liberal-conservative splits of the 1920s. These reasons include

1. The Christian's rejection of the naturalistic explanations of psychology
2. The Christian's difference with secular psychology's view of the human being
3. The Christian's rejection of the deterministic emphasis of psychology
4. The Christian's concern with personal responsibility
5. The Christian's differences with a secular view of sex
6. Theology's heavy emphasis on cognition and the Christian's tendency to remain aloof from strong emotions, especially intimacy and aggression

Other barriers lie more in the perspective of psychologists. Among these are

1. The psychologist's superficial understanding of Christianity and selected negative experiences with it
2. The psychologist's effort to establish a professional identity that is separate from philosophy and religion on the one hand and medicine and the natural sciences on the other

3. The psychologists' rejection of certain Christian presuppositions
4. Realities of time

Let us consider each of these barriers briefly.

THE CHRISTIAN CHURCH AND PSYCHOLOGY During the theological divisions of the 1920s, most denominations split into "liberal" and "conservative" elements. Each group went its own way. The evangelical wing of the church focused on concepts such as personal salvation, scriptural inerrancy, heaven and hell, and human depravity. The liberal church chose to minister to social needs. Both wings were concerned about the individual. For the conservative, the concern was primarily salvation. For the liberal, the emphasis was a social gospel.

In reacting to what they thought were negative emphases on hell, depravity, personal salvation, and the inerrancy of Scripture, the liberal wing of the church began to focus more on human potential and social action. Under the influence of German liberalism, they rebelled against a "pessimistic" view of the human being and began to hold out hope that through increased human effort workable solutions to humanity's dilemma would be found. As this segment of the church moved further from a focus on biblical theology and personal salvation, it turned increasingly to sociology, psychology, and politics as alternate means of ministering to the needs of society.

At the same time, the "conservative" wing of the church reaffirmed its commitment to the authority of Scripture and renewed its emphasis on personal salvation through the redemptive work of Christ. In doing so, this group disassociated itself from many areas of political or social concern exhibited by the "Liberals." Conservatives manifested a great deal of social outreach, but they limited it primarily to medical services, help for the down-and-outers, and assistance to members of local congregations.

In the 1920s a significant movement was quietly begun in the

Christian church. A man by the name of Anton Boisen published an article (1926/1971) challenging the church to become involved in people's emotional ills.

> We have therefore this truly remarkable situation—a church which has always been interested in the care of the sick, confining her efforts to the types of cases [physical] in which religion has least concern and least to contribute, while in those types in which it is impossible to tell where the domain of the medical worker leaves off and that of the religious worker begins [mental problems], there the church is doing nothing. (p. 9)

Boisen soon became a spokesman for those encouraging the church to minister to the emotional needs of society. By 1930 this new emphasis had gained so much ground that the Council for Clinical Pastoral Training was formed. This organization stimulated and coordinated new efforts in training ministers to help their people cope with their personal problems. Soon many seminaries were asking students to take short-term internships in mental hospitals as a means of becoming sensitive to psychological needs.

To all this the liberal church reacted favorably. Here was a way to minister to the inner needs of people. Psychology offered hope for the present world, not a pie-in-the-sky brand of Christian faith. In the thirties and forties, a distinct emphasis could be seen in the pastoral counseling movement, especially in the more liberal wing of the church. Under the influence of the writings of Sigmund Freud, pastors came to view people with problems as "sick" instead of sinful. Feelings of guilt and remorse were no longer necessarily seen as Christian virtues. They could also be the result of an inhibited upbringing that resulted in an overly strict superego (conscience). The goal of the pastor-counselor was no longer simply to lead people to accept God's forgiveness of their sins. Instead, the goal was to relax the strictness of these harsh superegos.

Well-known liberal theologians such as Harry Emerson Fosdick took up the banner of this new view of the human being. In *On Being a Real Person,* Fosdick (1943) endorsed the psychoanalytic view that neuroses arose, not from a lack of responsibility, but from an overly strict conscience.

> Indiscriminate praise of conscientiousness is psychologically
> dangerous. Many people worry themselves into complete disinte-
> gration over mere trifles and others have consciences so obtuse
> that they can get away with anything. (p. 133)

This thinking fit well with the liberal doctrine of the human
being. People with emotional problems were not necessarily de-
praved sinners. Instead, they were victims of their environment. The
solution to their ailments did not necessarily lie in a spiritual new
birth and consequent growth. Instead, it lay in an anthropocentric
growth process that needn't be concerned with supernatural phenomena.

During the 1940s a new influence came into American
psychology and was soon heartily endorsed by the liberal pastoral-
counseling movement. This was the "non-directive" or "client-
centered counseling" of Carl Rogers (1951). Rogers was raised in
what he described as a "strict religious environment," and he at-
tended Union Theological Seminary. His writings reflect a strong
rejection of the idea that humanity is basically sinful. Instead he
focuses on the innate tendency toward growth and actualization.
Given a healthy environment, people will throw off their negative
reactions and develop into healthy, fully functioning persons.

Based on these underlying presuppositions, Rogers's therapeutic method centered on providing the client a warm, accepting,
nonjudgmental atmosphere. Rather than giving directive advice to
persons in need of outside guidance, Rogers's client-centered
therapy encouraged clients to seek their own solutions. The counselor was no longer an expert or a guide; he was an accepting friend
who listened empathetically to the struggles of another human
being. This counseling method had great appeal to the liberal
church. Once again, it fit in with a positive view of the nature and
potential of the human being.

But neither psychoanalytic nor client-centered therapy had
much room for biblical insight or directive counsel. As pastoral
counseling began to rely increasingly on secular theories, the idea
that people were spiritual beings in need of salvation and spiritual
counsel progressively slipped into the background. As a matter of

fact, a counseling approach that gave much attention to specific biblical teaching seemed somehow suspect and unscientific. In the minds of the Liberals, strong reliance on scriptural teaching smacked of authoritarianism and the "fundamentalist mentality." Liberal theology was believed to have progressed beyond this narrow level.

In recent years two other forces have pressed into the forefront of psychological activity. These are existential philosophy and psychology on the one hand and behaviorism on the other. But while both of these perspectives occupy significant places in the psychological community, neither has yet made a major impact on the pastoral-counseling movement.

Each of these influences—the psychoanalytic, the Rogerian, the existentialist, and, more recently, the behavioral—have one thing in common: As philosophical systems, they have little room for a theology that focuses on biblical absolutes. And they have difficulty with the concepts of sin and personal salvation. Consequently, the liberal church's focus on personal adjustment and mental hygiene has in most cases been divorced from the teachings of the Bible and placed within the framework of a secular psychology. This is the great weakness of the liberal church's attempt to incorporate the insights of psychology into its ministry. It has no realistic hope of developing a unique perspective on psychology since it has largely abandoned the very concepts that can bring new life into psychology's understandings of the human being.

While discussing this development and the fact that many professional psychologists are now dissatisfied with their traditional psychotherapeutic approaches, O. Hobart Mowrer (1961) asks, "Has evangelical religion sold its birthright for a mess of psychological pottage?" (p. 60)[1] In other words, Mowrer, a secular psychologist, senses that much of the church has lost its potential contribution to psychology. Instead of offering some unique alternative perspectives, many Christians merely jump onto the psychological bandwagon.

---

[1]We suspect that Mowrer's use of the term "evangelical" is very broad and probably refers more to what the Evangelical would label "liberal."

While the liberal church was busy adopting a basically secular approach to personal adjustment and psychology, the evangelical church took a different tack. It steered clear of psychology. The pastoral counseling of the typical conservative minister was often very limited. And when he did counsel, it was usually following a conversion or in periods of death, grief, or special hardship. While many evangelical ministers were sensitive and supportive, the bulk of their counseling ministry was of a directive, Bible-teaching nature that failed to cope with many of the hidden wishes and frustrations of emotional living. The typical conservative minister was 20 or 30 years behind his liberal colleague in being aware of the contributions of psychology to the understanding of personality. We turn now to a discussion of some of the apparent reasons for this lag.

The Rejection of Naturalism

A primary reason for the Evangelical's failure to encounter psychological science concerned the influence of the supernatural. Psychology, of course, was deeply committed to naturalistic explanations. If it were to build a science of behavior, it would have to have a set of laws. It would have to be able to accurately predict behavior given all the variables. At the same time, Christianity was committed to a biblical supernaturalism. Many Christians assumed that if psychologists could explain and modify human behavior without reference to spiritual principles, the whole concept of the supernatural was in question. In fact, they could even point to the liberal wing of the church as an example of what happened when one adopted the naturalistic views of psychology.

The Rejection of Non-Christian Views of the Human Being

Every psychological theory makes assumptions about the nature of the human being and human dilemmas. Many of these assumptions are clearly contrary to biblical affirmations and have met with disapproval in the Christian community. For example, the influence of Carl Rogers and similar humanistic theoreticians on Evangelicals has been limited, because of their emphasis on human "goodness" and their therapeutic method. Adams (1970) states:

> The Rogerian system confirms sinful man's belief that he is au-
> tonomous and has no need of God. Conservatives must reject
> Rogerian counseling on the basis of its humanistic presuppositions
> alone. It begins with man and it ends with man. Man is his own
> solution to his problems. (p. 82)

To a doctrinally oriented, Bible-teaching movement, the idea
of sitting quietly and empathizing with the needs of people was
difficult enough to swallow. Add to this the view that people are
essentially good and you can see how out of line with the traditional
evangelical approach Rogers's views would be.

The Rejection of Determinism

Closely related to the Christian's concern with psychology's
naturalistic assumptions is another aspect of psychology's view of
the human being. This is the concern with psychology's emphasis
on determinism. As a science, psychology must operate on the
assumption that we live in a cause-and-effect world. But for
Christians, the concept of cause and effect stirs up concern over free
will, determinism, and personal responsibility.

Christians especially respond to the complete philosophical
determinism of psychologists such as Skinner. For example, after
summarizing the traditional view that human freedom prevails over
external controls, Skinner writes:

> This escape route is slowly closed as new evidences of the pre-
> dictability of human behavior are discovered. Personal exemption
> from a complete determinism is revoked as a scientific analysis
> progresses, particularly in accounting for the behavior of the indi-
> vidual.
>
> In questioning the control exercised by autonomous man and
> demonstrating the control exercised by the environment, a sci-
> ence of behavior also seems to question dignity or worth. A per-
> son is responsible for his behavior, not only in the sense that he
> may be justly blamed or punished when he behaves badly, but
> also in the sense that he is to be given credit and admired for his
> achievements. A scientific analysis shifts the credit as well as the
> blame to the environment, and traditional practices can then no
> longer be justified. These are sweeping changes, and those who
> are committed to traditional theories and practices naturally resist
> them. (pp. 19-21)

Unfortunately, both theologians and psychologists have frequently added to their mutual suspicion by failing to distinguish between determinism as a working hypothesis necessary for the progress of science and philosophical determinism. Meehl (1958) suggests the following threefold distinction:

> 1. *Methodological determinism.* "Let us seek pertinaciously for the laws which we hope, and expect, will be exhibited by any given domain of behavior. If these laws hold strictly, well and good; if they are at best probabilistic, we will settle for that, since they will still be very useful."
>
> 2. *Empirical determinism.* "Since the quest proposed in (1) has been fairly successful thus far, it seems likely that all behavior domains do, in fact, follow such exceptionless regularities. Apparent exceptions are very probably due to incomplete information and, pending further investigation, will be assumed to be such."
>
> 3. *Metaphysical determinism.* "All human psychological events instantialize universal laws, and we hold this thesis as an absolute ontological presupposition which no empirical evidence could be permitted to gainsay." (p. 81)

It seems that no Christian need quarrel with "methodological determinism." If God is the Creator and there is an order to His creation, we should expect to find a great deal of lawfulness and regularity in every area of creation. Indeed, if there is no regularity and predictability, there is no foundation for any scientific study and we are left with an irrational or at least nonintelligible world.

Christianity's problems with determinism begin with empirical determinism and become especially strong with metaphysical determinism. But are the latter really essential to the study of psychology? If all behavior is mechanistically determined, it is true that we will never have a complete psychology unless we operate on this assumption. However, if God does intervene in human history, and if a human being does have any measure of personal freedom, a psychological study based on metaphysical determinism never arrives at a proper understanding of the universe. An alternative to metaphysical determinism will be essential if we are to come to a right understanding of the nature of reality.

Christianity's Concern With Personal Responsibility

Another fear of the conservatives was that when people understood the causes of human behavior, they would no longer hold themselves responsible for their actions. Psychotherapy, especially psychoanalytically oriented therapy, was seen as an attempt to set people free of their inhibitions, turning them into impulsive, irresponsible sinners, and to rid them of the concept of personal responsibility.

In words common to the antipsychological stance of many Christian writers, Adams (1970) states: *He's not our spokesman*

> The idea of sickness as the cause of personal problems vitiates all notions of human responsibility. This is the crux of the matter. People no longer consider themselves responsible for what they do wrong. Instead they blame society—"ours is a sick society," they say. Others specifically blame grandmother, mother, the church, a school teacher, or some other particular individual for their actions. Freudian psychoanalysis itself turns out to be an archeological expedition back into the past in which a search is made for others on whom to pin the blame for our behavior. The fundamental idea is to find out how others have wronged us. It should not be difficult to see how irresponsibility is the upshot of such an emphasis and how many of the domestic and world-wide problems we face in our time are directly related to it. (pp. 5-6)

Although many would reject Adams's caricature of psychoanalysis, it is clear that this image of psychoanalytic theory has been the basis for the rejection of the insights of psychology in the minds of many Christians.

More recently, Christianity's concern with the psychic determinism of psychoanalysis has been replaced by a concern over the deterministic emphasis of behaviorism and its therapeutic offspring—behavior modification. In commenting on James Dobson's use of some behavioral principles, Adams (1973) writes:

> When [he], for instance, recommends strictly behavioristic methods for child raising in the name of Christianity, he badly confuses important distinctions and erases lines that forever must be drawn clearly. His near total capitulation to behaviorism is couched in Christian terms but really introduces an equally god-

less system into the Christian home while purporting to be a Christian reaction to permissiveness. (p. 82)

Without beginning a debate on the effects of either psychoanalysis or behaviorism on personal responsibility in our society, it will suffice to say that the emphasis on psychic determinism in psychology and the fear among many Christians that psychological explanations will lead to irresponsibility have been major barriers to attempts at integration.

Psychology's Emphasis on Sex

The centrality of sexual impulses in Freudian theory was a red flag to many conservatives. They feared that therapeutic approaches linking the inhibition of sexual desires with neurosis would undermine the ethical demands of Scripture and thereby lower moral standards. This was a sure sign that psychology (at least the psychoanalytic version) was "of the devil" and had nothing to offer a biblical Christian.

Without going into in-depth study, it appears that there is some truth in this view. From a biblical perspective Freud's view of the human being does leave much to be desired, and some therapists have promoted sexual "acting out." At the same time, it is equally apparent that Christianity has often been guilty of promoting a repressive, unrealistic view of sex. The history of the church's views on sexuality leaves much to be desired and has led one writer (Small, 1974) to comment:

> The history of Christian thought on the subject of sexuality is a long, dark journey. The story, while at best intriguing, at worst is downright dismal. Contemporary young minds must find it incredulous. Prior to the beginning of our own century it cannot be termed in any true sense positive. (p. 46)

Small goes on to mention facts such as Augustine's view that since the sex act included an element of lust, the true Christian "would prefer to beget children without this kind of lust." He also notes Origen's belief that all sexual activity was inherently wrong and the ground of all actual sins. With this sort of background, one suspects that the church's strong negative reaction to Freud's views on sex was motivated by more than a firm commitment to biblical truth. In fact, his own hypotheses about repression and reaction formation may well explain some of the church's angry attacks on Freud. In any case, we can certainly see the barrier this view erected between psychology and Christianity.

Theology's Cognitive Focus

Throughout the history of the Christian church theologians have focused on the accurate statement of theological beliefs, often to the exclusion of theorizing on the role of emotions and the development of personality in the Christian life. There are probably several reasons for this focus.

One is the fact that theological thinkers tend to be just that—thinkers. Their primary call is not pastoring but theologizing; consequently, they focus more on cognitive issues, ideas, and the history of thought than on the development of personality. As important as accurate theological statements are, however, they can be overemphasized at the expense of the emotional and the interpersonal sides of living. Both Kierkegaard's radical reaction to nineteenth-century liberal rationalism and the current emphasis on relational theology are reactions against excessively cognitive emphases in the church.

A second cause for theology's strong cognitive focus may lie in the defensive processes so familiar to dynamically oriented psychologists. Feelings can be frightening. Intense love, moods of depression, outbursts of anger, and the needs for support are carefully avoided by many people. For Christians especially, there is the fear that love will turn to lust or discouragement to despair. Sensing the turmoil of these strong emotions, it may be that some pastors and theologians have felt more comfortable focusing on people's belief systems and external behavior than they have on inner attitudes and feelings.

In fact, many Christian subcultures have a distinctively nonemotional basis. Christians are told they should be happy; so they smile (even though they hurt inside). They are told Christians should be loving; so they try to act lovingly (without paying any attention to their feelings). And they are told Christians should be saintly; so they put on an outward show of piety (while strong emotions—often negative—are raging inside).

An example of the negation of emotion found in many evangelical and fundamental circles is the use of a railroad as a parallel to the Christian life. We are told that the engine is fact (the Bible), the next car is faith (trust in God's Word), and the caboose is feeling. This train must obviously be pulled by the engine of fact and followed by faith. It will run with or without the caboose!

While we agree that major decisions in life should be based on the Word of God, sound counsel, and Christian reason, this analogy tends to picture emotions as a nuisance factor in the Christian life. In fact, the impression is sometimes given that we would be better off without emotions because they lead to subjective, feeling-oriented decisions that muddy the waters of consistent Christian living. In contrast to this, the apostle Paul wrote:

> If we are distressed, it is for your comfort and salvation; if we are comforted, it is for your comfort, which produces in you patient endurance of the same sufferings we suffer. And our hope for you is firm, because we know that just as you share in our sufferings, so also you share in our comfort. We do not want you to be uninformed, brothers, about the hardships we suffered in the province of Asia. We were under great pressure, far beyond our ability to endure, so that we despaired even of life. (2 Cor. 1:6-8)

Other manifestations of the fear of feelings and of intimacy are found in our Christian literature and hymnology. One well-known hymn asks, "Are you weary, are you heavy hearted? Tell it to Jesus alone." Are we to understand this to mean the following? "Don't share your problems with another person. Hold it in. Hide your needs and tell it to Jesus alone." What a contrast this isolationistic view of the Christian life is to passages such as the following:

> Carry each other's burdens, and in this way you will fulfill the law of Christ. (Gal. 6:2)

> Therefore confess your sins to each other and pray for each other so that you may be healed. The prayer of a righteous man is powerful and effective. (James 5:16)

> Therefore encourage one another and build each other up, just as
> in fact you are doing. (1 Thess. 5:11)

This fearful avoidance of feelings and intimacy in the Christian life has encouraged many to erect or maintain rigid barriers against deep involvement with other persons and has caused others to approach Christian service as an obligation rather than the natural result of living a fulfilling life. It has caused many to steer clear of any involvement with psychology for fear of contaminating a pure, "objective," intellectualized theology with the "subjective" content of inner human nature. In fact, this issue cuts to the heart of many conflicts between psychologists and theologians. Most of those who work in interdisciplinary settings, including those in both theological and psychological institutions, will be well aware of the tensions that arise over this issue. Theologians are frequently chided by their psychological colleagues as being too cognitive, abstract, or intellectual while psychologists are accused of being too subjective or too feeling oriented. While generalizations are always dangerous, one suspects there may often be truth in both of these assertions.

Summary

We can now see why the church has largely failed to make distinctive contributions to psychology and why the church has not profited as it might from psychology's study of the human being. At the expense of ministering to the emotional needs of man, the evangelical church has focused primarily on the need for personal salvation, doctrinal orthodoxy, and moral purity. Its social emphasis has been mainly in the realm of physical needs, and a series of important conflicts with psychology have held Evangelicals back from the potential contributions of psychology.

At the same time, the more liberal wing of the church has failed to make substantial contributions to integration because it has moved from its biblical moorings and adopted an essentially secular psychology. Consequently, neither group is actively applying the vast resources of scriptural teachings to the daily personal needs of the average person or to the academic study of psychology.

PSYCHOLOGY AND CHRISTIANITY

But we cannot lay the blame for the failure to develop a sufficiently integrated view of the human being entirely at the feet of the Christian community. Secular psychologists, too, have played their part in isolationism. We will look at some reasons for the hesitance of psychologists to join with Christians in an effort to gain a broadened view of the human being.

Superficial Understanding of the Christian Faith

As a starter, few psychologists who theorize about the nature of the human being are actively religious. Many have had only superficial contact with biblical Christianity while others have had a very negative encounter. For example, consider the psychotherapist who has counseled a number of Christian patients, each suffering from a deep sense of worthlessness and guilt. These clients naturally relate these feelings to their Christian experience. They think their guilt and condemnation come directly from the Lord. And they have a terribly hard time throwing off the shackles of inferiority and disesteem. Sometimes they go so far as to justify their self-hatred as being consistent with biblical principles of humility or self-denial.

And what is the nonreligious therapist to conclude? A natural response is that religion is a destructive force causing people to feel worthless and guilty. Add to this a brief encounter with the term "total depravity" and our psychologist is sure that religious faith attempts to sabotage mental health by instilling deep feelings of guilt and fear.

Another aspect of the secular psychologist's difficulty in comprehending the Christian view of the human being is the fact that certain perceptions of truth and reality are not open to the nonbeliever. The apostle Paul wrote concerning believers and nonbelievers:

> We have not received the spirit of the world but the Spirit who is from God, that we may understand what God has freely given us. This is what we speak, not in words taught us by human wisdom but in words taught by the Spirit, expressing spiritual truths in spiritual words. The man without the Spirit does not accept the things that come from the Spirit of God, for they are foolishness to

him, and he cannot understand them, because they are spiritually
discerned. (1 Cor. 2:12-14)

Paul makes it clear that there is a wisdom that the person who
does not possess a personal relationship with Christ cannot possess.
It is impossible for the unregenerate person to comprehend some
aspects of truth. In spite of great personal sensitivity and insight, the
non-Christian psychologist has a limited vision of the condition of
humanity. Some conflicts in views of the nature of the human being
and human functioning are due to this lack of perception by the
non-Christian.

At this point we should, however, add a word of caution. Some
Christians have a way of writing off every difference of opinion with
non-Christians to their "lack of spiritual discernment." While this is
sometimes true, the misunderstanding is frequently as much the
fault of our own inadequate understanding or our failure to com-
municate. We tend to clutter up the Christian message with our own
brand of Christian subculture and cloud over a clear picture of
biblical truth. In these cases we need to help our non-Christian
colleagues cut through these externals to the core of biblical truth.
Many of these persons are open-minded and are ready to dialogue
on substantive issues that are presented clearly.

The Psychologist's Identity

As a discipline, psychology is approximately one hundred years old.
Compared to the natural sciences, psychology is young and has had
a hard time finding its scientific niche. The inner workings of the
mind have a tint of the subjective, which is an alien word to
experimental scientists. To overcome the suspicion that it is not
truly scientific, psychology has had to make determined efforts to
establish itself in the mainstream of the scientific world. To do this,
it has chosen to accept and to emphasize the major tenets and
methods of objective science. Included, of course, is a rigid adher-
ence to the scientific method and to naturalistic assumptions about
the universe.

Based on this philosophy, graduate programs in psychology
ignore the possibility of supernatural phenomena and extra-

empirical sources of truth. Trained in these types of programs, a prospective psychologist cannot easily escape adopting a similar attitude toward biblical revelation and supernatural phenomena. The religious devotee is seen as either naive, dependent, or unscientific, and possibly as all three.

This problem is compounded by the fact that psychologists have viewed their discipline as an experimental rather than a philosophical one. This means that in obtaining a doctorate in psychology one is trained in research, statistics, and empirical methods. It is data or research that really counts. The American Psychological Association publishes only one journal that accepts purely theoretical papers. And only in the last few years has it become possible to write a nonexperimental doctoral dissertation in clinical psychology.

By definition Christian concepts such as God, grace, and salvation do not lend themselves to empirical research. Consequently, those who argue for the reality of God on historical, philosophical, or biblical grounds are likely to find their arguments dismissed as irrelevant philosophical speculation that is beyond the scope of scientific psychology.

Conflicting Presuppositions

In previous pages, we have looked at several presuppositions that pose problems for the Christian who approaches the findings of psychology. Without being repetitive, we can merely say that psychologists, too, are bothered by certain Christian suppositions. Supernaturalism, free will, and the concept of people as sinners give many psychologists problems and tend to erect barriers to meaningful dialogue and interaction.

Realities of Time

But these factors alone do not account for the hesitancy of psychologists to join in an integrative encounter. The practical realities of time and competence make it difficult for the average person to master one discipline effectively, let alone take the time to recognize and understand the viewpoints and teachings of a related profession. Even well-meaning, open-minded professionals are limited in their ability to dialogue intelligently with colleagues in other disciplines.

With the increasing body of knowledge in psychology, graduate programs are becoming longer. Nonclinical doctoral programs require at least three years of full-time postcollege study. And clinical and counseling doctorates require an additional year of internship. This means that a person has spent twenty years in school before receiving a doctorate in psychology and being ready to begin a career. Theological training is equally as rigorous and in some instances requires six years of postcollege education for a doctorate.

With these requirements, it is little wonder that few people have the time or energy to undertake a serious integration of psychology and theology. On top of this, most of our educational institutions are not designed to promote interdisciplinary study. Majors are offered in narrow academic specializations with relatively few electives, and this also works against the possibility of integrating one's Christian view of life with a secular academic discipline.

SUMMARY This concludes our survey of some of the barriers to a meaningful dialogue between psychology and theology. These barriers form a background for our discussion of different approaches to integration in chapters 4 through 7. But before we turn to those models of integration, we want to sketch some of the possibilities for integration and a few of the many areas of significant overlap between the data of psychology and Scripture. This is our task in chapter 3.

THE SCOPE
OF INTEGRATION

In this chapter we want to **3** expand the scope of the integration of psychological and theological conceptions of human functioning by look- ing at the overlap between a number of theological concerns and statements and their counterparts in psychology. Several assumptions undergird these comparisons:

1. All truth is God's truth. Consequently, the truths of psychology are not contradictory to the truths of divine revelation; in fact, they have the potential of being integrated into a harmonious whole.
2. Theology represents the distillation of God's revelation of Himself to humanity in a linguistic, conceptual, and cultural medium people can understand.
3. This revelation focuses primarily on human nature and human destiny in God's program.
4. Psychology is primarily concerned with the mechanisms by which people function and the methods to assess and influence that functioning.

49

5. As such, the content of psychology provides a statement on the nature and functioning of humanity.

Building on these assumptions, we suggest that there are common features that are intrinsic to the content of both psychology and theology. To demonstrate these common features we will begin by outlining the overlapping concerns addressed by psychology and one division of theological study, namely that of systematic theology. This extensive overlap is some of the major territory for the integration of psychology and theology.

SYSTEMATIC THEOLOGY AND PSYCHOLOGY Every discipline must, at one time or another, formulate its data and its theories into some framework, organizational outline, or structure. Without this way of ordering facts and theories, we have only disjointed bits of information that are essentially unrelatable to other data. While the organizational framework each discipline selects is arbitrary, it does provide the structure and cohesiveness needed to pursue an orderly study of particular phenomena.

Systematic theology and psychology are no exception. Both have been conceptualized according to a variety of outlines, organizations, and schemata. While the order and nomenclature of these schemata vary somewhat from author to author, the content is basically the same.[1] Table 2 contains a rather typical outline of systematic theology.[2] Table 3 presents an outline of the scope of psychology chosen to demonstrate the broad range of common concerns of psychology and theology.

---

[1] We are indebted to Richard Mohline for his contributions to the development of the concepts presented in this section.

[2] Areas not explicitly covered in this model include the theological teachings on angels and demons and the psychological study of parapsychological phenomena. Theology traditionally discusses angelology under the general topic of theology proper, especially the works of God. While we have not attempted to approach the difficult question of either angels or psychic phenomenon, we suspect that a mutual biblical and psychological approach to these concepts could also be fruitful for integration.

TABLE 2—THE SCOPE OF SYSTEMATIC THEOLOGY

Theology Proper	Prolegomena (definitions, the nature and necessity of theology, divisions of theology and presuppositions) Theism (definitions and existence of God) Bibliology (scriptural revelation and inspiration) Theology (the nature, decrees, and works of God)
Anthropology	Origin (the creation of the human being) Nature, Character, and Functioning of the Human Being Fall (the introduction of sin into the human race)
Hamartiology	Nature (the definition and essential principle of sin) Universality Origin Imputation Consequences
Soteriology	Election and Calling Faith Justification Regeneration Adoption Conversion Sanctification Repentance Perseverance
Christology and Pneumatology	Incarnation Person of Christ Offices of Christ Hypostatic Union
Ecclesiology	Meaning (the doctrine and definition of the church) Nature Founding Ordinances Relationships and Leadership
Eschatology	Second Coming Resurrections Judgments Millennium Final State

TABLE 3—THE SCOPE OF PSYCHOLOGY

Science of Psychology	Foundations of Psychology Definitions Presuppositions and Methods
Personality Theory	Nature, Character, and Functioning of the Human Being (including learning, perception, memory, and emotion)
Psychopathology (abnormal psychology)	Nature, Origin and Consequences of Pathological Functioning
Developmental Psychology	Stages of Growth and Concepts of Maturity
Counseling	Personality, preparation, and role of the counselor
Social Psychology	Social Organization Nature of Groups Formation of Groups and Attitudes Interpersonal Dynamics Leadership
Psychology of Motivation*	Goals Expectations Rewards

A look at Tables 2 and 3 demonstrates the extensive commonality of content area within both psychology and theology. Before elaborating on these basic common areas, however, it should be pointed out that there are some major differences of approach to and explanation of the common content areas. To begin with, the locus of explanation is different in theology and psychology. In theology, the locus of explanation is generally historical and sociocultural, while in psychology it is descriptive (clinical), developmental, and experimental. Secondly, the level of explanation is different. In theology, the level of explanation is metaphysical. In

*Here we deal only with a limited aspect of motivation. A consideration of drive theory could be included under personality theory and motivational aspects of motivation under developmental psychology.

psychology, the level of explanation is empirical or scientific. Finally, there is a difference of epistemology. Theology's epistemology is revelational while psychology's epistemology is empirical.

In spite of these differences, a commitment to the belief that there is a unity of truth suggests that psychology and theology are still integrative. Since Scripture is metaphysical and revelational in character, theology tends to be more comprehensive than psychology in locus of explanation, level of explanation, and epistemology. We are proposing that the common content and principles outlined in Tables 2 and 3 constitute one way of viewing the scope of the integration of psychology and theology. Although the nature, character, and levels of the integrable material vary from area to area, we believe that the basic principles and content of psychology can be integrated into their equivalent theological areas. Although many other outlines could be chosen for both psychology and theology, these are selected for illustrative purposes.

Without attempting to be exhaustive, we will now take a brief look at some of the possibilities for integration in each of these common areas. Then we will raise a number of questions that must be addressed in the development of a truly Christian viewpoint on psychology or in a theology that speaks comprehensively to the concerns of humanity. In some areas the overlap is minimal. Psychology offers no direct counterpart, for example, to theology's discussion of the existence and nature of God (unless, of course, we parallel certain aspects of personality theory that deal with psychology's attempts to explain the origin of humanity's God-concepts). And eschatology (the doctrine of last things) has few parallels to the traditional subject matter of psychology. But the minimal overlap in these areas simply reveals that theology has traditionally been conceptualized in a more comprehensive manner than psychology.

Theology Proper / Psychology as Science

All disciplines operate from a basic set of implicit or explicit assumptions or presuppositions. Psychology and theology are no exception. Both begin with a statement of assumptions or propositions regarding the nature of their subject matter, their methodology, and their working hypotheses. It is here, in the underlying presuppositions, that the differences in scope and methodology and most of the apparent conflicts between psychology and theology have their roots. Because some of theology's assumptions diverge from those of psychology, the stage is set for conflict further down the road.

For example, consider the realm of epistemology. Most psychologists begin with the assumption that empiricism is the only valid means for arriving at scientific knowledge. Theologians, however, while not necessarily rejecting the validity of either scientific empiricism or philosophic rationalism, operate on the assumption that there is a third source of knowledge—revelation. Whether it is faith in the revelation of Scripture or faith in the reality of a personal encounter with God, the Christian affirms that there is a source of knowledge beyond those of rationalism and empiricism.

Whereas psychology typically begins with a discussion of the usefulness of the scientific method, the nature of experimentation, and the nature of empirical laws, theologians generally begin their studies with certain affirmations regarding the existence of God and His revelation through Christ and Scripture. J. Oliver Buswell (1962) writes: "The primary presupposition of the Christian religion is, of course, Jesus Christ. This means . . . that we presuppose the sovereign Triune God of the Bible, and we presuppose the Bible or the infallible Word of God" (p. 15). This assumption leads naturally to a certain view of reality and of the appropriate means of comprehending this reality.

Thus, although some of the presuppositions of psychology and theology are different (and sometimes in conflict), there is a formal similarity in that both theology proper and the science or philosophy of psychology speak to underlying methodological and preliminary issues that are basic to the study of the rest of their discipline. A study of these issues helps clarify some of the essential similarities and differences between psychology and theology and can help us avoid some apparent conflicts by recognizing that the two disciplines frequently are addressing issues from different levels of explanation and from different methodological bases. An understanding of these issues can also help us avoid forced or artificial attempts at integration when differing focuses or levels of interpretation are in focus. Some of the questions that need to be addressed in the study of both theology proper and psychology as a science include:

1. What sources of knowledge will be appealed to in our study of persons?
2. What methods are acceptable in gathering the information?
3. What classes of explanatory hypothesis are valid in attempting to explain the knowledge we do have?
4. What level of explanation is appropriate to account for the human being's fundamental nature? For example, do basic (lower-level) physiological processes account for higher psychological processes such as consciousness? Or is the reverse true?
5. What is the relationship of revelation to rational and empirical methods of science?
6. In what way is the formal (methodological) integration between theology proper and the science of psychology similar and different from the other areas of integration?

Anthropology / Personality Theory

Biblical anthropology is the branch of systematic theology dealing with the origin and nature of the human being. It is, of course, one of the most important areas for those studying the relationship of psychology and theology. A Christian understanding of personality begins with the biblical affirmation that each person is created in the image and likeness of God (Gen. 1:27). Questions on the composition of human nature, the soul, and freedom and responsibility are, for the Christian, ultimately answerable only within the framework of this biblical affirmation. Autonomous humans in isolation from God may amass all sorts of information about the human being; but without seeing persons in relation to God, we cannot know them as they truly are and as they were fully meant to be. Berkhouwer (1962) put it this way:

> Anyone who tries to construct a picture of man or of himself without the light of divine revelation can never obtain anything

except a picture in which the unique nature of man does not appear. . . . The relation of man's nature to God is not something which is added to an already complete, self enclosed, isolated nature; it is essential and constitutive for man's nature, and man cannot be understood apart from this relation. Only an abstract view of man, which ignores this relationship, can abstract or separate the knowledge of man from the knowledge of God—with the unavoidable result that such "knowledge" becomes abstract, and no longer refers to actual man, real man, man as he really is. (pp. 21-23)

But the human being in the image of God is only one side of the biblical picture. The fall of the human race into sin also has broad implications for our understanding of personality. After stating that sin prevents any human being from realizing complete psychological balance during their earthly existence, Schaeffer (1971) observes:

Now into this situation comes the modern non-Christian psychologist, trying to bring an integration into the thought world. But the non-Christian psychologist, by the very nature of what he believes, will try to bring about an integration on the level of the original rebellion. . . . As a result, the integration will be an attempt to relate what is broken in the person to the animals and the machines or it will ask for a romantic leap. (p. 129)

For the Christian, then, the dual facts of humanity created in the image of God and the human race as fallen constitute the framework of our view of personality. It is from these roots that we build our understanding of persons—their essence, their dignity and worth, their conflicts, and ultimately their growth and renewal.

Turning to personality theory (within which we include the basic processes of learning, perception, memory, and emotion), it is evident that every personality theory is an implicit statement of the nature of the human being. Every personality theory makes assumptions about human nature, the foundations of personality, and the nature and sources of personal maladjustments. Skinner (1971), for example, writes:

Science does not dehumanize man, it de-homunculizes him, and it must do so if it is to prevent the abolition of the human species. To man *qua* man we readily say good riddance. Only by depossessing him can we turn to the real causes of human behavior. Only then can we turn from the inferred to the observed, from the miraculous to the natural, from the inaccessible to the manipulable.

It is often said that in doing so we must treat the man who survives as a mere animal. "Animal" is a pejorative term, but only because "man" has been made spuriously horrific. Krutch has argued that whereas the traditional view supports Hamlet's exclamation "How like a god!", Pavlov, the behavioral scientist, emphasized, "How like a dog!" But that was a step forward. A god is the archetypal pattern of an explanatory fiction, of a miracle-working mind, of the metaphysical. Man is much more than a dog, but like a dog he is within range of a scientific analysis. (pp. 200-201)

And Fenichel (1945), author of one of the major psychoanalytic textbooks on psychopathology, writes:

Scientific psychology explains mental phenomena as a result of the interplay of primitive physical needs—rooted in the biological structure of man and developed in the course of biological history—and the influence of the environment on these needs. There is no place for any other factor. (p. 5)

These well-known representatives are expressing their conception of the nature of the human being. The Christian will take issue with this reduction of the human to the physical and animal realms. Yet at the same time, we must offer in its place an understanding of the human being that embraces both the physiological, animallike, and determined aspects of human nature as well as the immaterial, godlike, and free and responsible aspects of the human personality.

Several attempts have been made to categorize personality theorists according to their underlying assumptions. Rychlak (1972), for example, describes behaviorally oriented theories as Lockean, phenomenological or existential theories as Kantian, and analytic theories as a mixture of the two. But whatever the model, it is evident that personality theories, however much they differ in content, all make implicit or explicit assumptions about the nature of the human being and are therefore psychologies equivalent to biblical anthropology.

In developing a holistic view of personality that includes the data of both biblical revelation and psychological science several questions must be comprehensively addressed. These include:

1. To what extent is the human being similar to and different from animals?
2. What is the meaning and significance of the biblical affirmation that the human being is created in the image of God?
3. Can human behavior be reduced to the purely physiological (materialistic monism), and, if not, how are we to understand the spiritual or immaterial side?
4. To what extent is a person a free and responsible human being?
5. Is there any similarity between spiritual and psychological maturity?
6. Is the biblical model of the human being (following Rychlak, 1972), more Kantian, Lockean, mixed, or none of these?
7. Is the concept of a soul (and/or a spirit) the same as the psyche or psychological functioning?

Hamartiology / Psychopathology

Every discipline must struggle to understand and explain the misery of the human being. There is no getting around the fact that something radical has gone amiss in the human personality. Both individually and corporately we encounter problems of gigantic proportion. Theology addresses this problem under the nature, scope, and effects of sin (hamartiology). Theories of personality discuss this problem under the nature, scope, and effects of psychopathology. Both speak to lowered functioning, loss of potential, and/or inappropriate behavior of the human personality.

Theologically, humanity's sin or fallen condition is frequently discussed in a fourfold manner. Theologians speak of: (a) depravity, (b) penalty or condemnation, (c) alienation, and (d) guilt. These four states or human conditions parallel certain specific psychological experiences associated with psychopathology and should be integrable with them. The concept of depravity focuses on the corruption or disturbance of all aspects of the divine image in humanity. It refers to the fact that every area of personal being is somehow influenced by the presence of sin in the human race. Human existence under the sentence of death or penalty for rebellion is integrable with the psychological experiences of fear and anxiety. Theologically, human anxiety relates to the fact that people are in a state of condemnation. Humankind's alienation from God and consequently from themselves and others speaks to the problem of loneliness and isolation. And our condition of guilt before God relates to our experience of psychological guilt. Every area of theology's understanding of sin, therefore, can be shown to relate to the conditions of personal maladjustment that applied psychologists are addressing.

One of the basic questions to be answered in relating the concepts of sin and psychopathology to one another is that of cause and effect. Most psychologists view what Christians call sin as psychopathology—or the results of it. In other words, they see what the Christian calls "sin" as a *result* of emotional disturbance—not a *cause*. Seeing the roots of "sin" in early life experiences, they frequently have difficulty reconciling their findings to the biblical concepts of personal freedom and responsibility.

On the other hand, Christians who view all psychopathology as being the result of sin often have difficulty relating their theological concept of sin to the data and theories of psychology. Any satisfactory Christian view of the human being will have to resolve or at least speak to this seeming contradiction. And in doing so, it will have to answer questions such as the following:

1. What is the essence and cause of sin?
2. What is the essence and cause of psychopathology?
3. What is the relationship between personal responsibility and societal and parental responsibility?
4. Is there a difference between the results of direct, conscious, willful sin and unconscious sins, and if so, what are the implications of these differences?

5. Why are some nonbelievers relatively healthy (psychologically) while some believers are relatively unhealthy (psychologically)?

6. What is the relationship between *being* a sinner (fallen human nature) and *sinning* as it relates to being pathological and acting pathologically?

7. Is it necessary to have a conception of inner structure and process either biblically or psychologically in order to account for wrong action either biblically or psychologically?

Soteriology / Developmental Psychology

After developing a view of personality consistent with biblical anthropology and a view of psychopathology that incorporates scriptural revelation on the nature and effects of sin, there arises the need to build a theory of personality development that is consistent with the Christian understanding of salvation and personal growth. Systematic theology traditionally discusses these concepts under the doctrine of soteriology (salvation). Here theologians discuss concepts such as election, calling, regeneration, conversion, repentance, faith, adoption, justification, sanctification, and perseverance. Each of these concepts refers to one or more aspects of the work of God (and our response to it) in reconciling sinful people first of all to Himself and also to themselves and to fellow human beings.

To the degree that these concepts, culminating in the concept of sanctification, refer to changes within one's personality, they should be integrable with both child growth and development (developmental psychology) and client growth and development (therapeutic psychology). A look at the implications of a few of these subdoctrines in the order of salvation illustrates some of the potential areas of fruitful interaction between theological and psychological understandings of personality growth and development.

Theologically, the concept of election is used to express the belief that those who become the people of God do so because of the free decision of God. *Calling* refers to the process in which God, speaking by the Holy Spirit and through the Word, calls out of bondage to sin those He has elected. Consequently, both calling and election speak of a source of life and growth grounded in another person and carrying with it a sense of significance and value that is not conditionally based. Just as election and calling are starting points in the order of salvation, so, dynamically, a cornerstone of all personality growth is the sense of significance that is rooted in the knowledge that one has been chosen (by a parent or by a therapist) apart from one's performance.

The doctrines of regeneration and conversion refer to that radical moment when those created in God's image, but fallen into a state of alienation from God and self, experience a new beginning. They receive spiritual life (the new birth) and enter a new phase where they can, through the experience of grace, progressively overcome both the division within their personality and their separation from God and others.

Christian conversion refers to a change from one state to another—from the state of dissonance or alienation from God to a state of harmony with God. Theologically this alienation is based on human assertion of autonomy and rejection of the authority of God. In sin, people assert their independence and attempt to be "like God." In other words, they set themselves up as God. This denial of creatureliness is paralleled by the neurotic's continued search to be something one is not (see Horney [1950]). In regeneration and conversion, humans acknowledge their dependency, repent of their autonomous self-direction, and place faith or trust in God. This accepting of finiteness and accompanying repentance and faith lay the foundation for overcoming the split in human personality—the gap between who we are and who we want to be. Only as we acknowledge the uselessness of a continued search for autonomous self-achievement and fulfillment and accept the fact of our creatureliness can we begin to come to grips with our true potential.

Justification is the theological term used to describe God's gracious act of pardoning all of our sins and accepting us as righteous in His sight on the basis of Christ's sinless life and substitutionary death. In regeneration we receive new life spiritually and a new nature. In justification we receive a new standing (just as though we never sinned). The New Testament concept of adoption literally means "placing as a son." It communicates the fact that Christians have been placed in the family of God in such a way as to receive all the benefits that Jesus, as the Son of God, has at His disposal. As adoptive children, we become heirs of the Father and joint heirs with His Son (Rom. 8:17). For Christians the facts of justification and adoption provide a deep and lasting resource for the solution to problems of guilt and self-acceptance. God's pardon of our sins provides the ultimate basis for resolving the problem of guilt that is at the heart of every emotional maladjustment. And the unconditional acceptance reflected in being adopted as God's children provides a foundation on which we can erect much-needed attitudes of self-acceptance. If God accepts us exactly as we are, how dare we not learn to accept ourselves regardless of our failures?

The crucial psychotherapeutic value of acceptance certainly parallels the divine acceptance evidenced in God's acts of justification and adoption. Just as a believer's unconditional acceptance by God is the freeing and motivating source for Christian growth and maturity, so the therapeutic experience of personal acceptance forms the soil from which most client growth proceeds. In a similar manner, a parent's unconditional acceptance is absolutely necessary to the development of a young child's personality.

The theological concept of perseverance refers to the belief that no one who has been justified by God's grace and regenerated by the Holy Spirit will fall away from this state of grace, but will instead persevere to salvation (Hodge, 1872/1960). This doctrine speaks directly to the issue of security and has clear-cut psychological implications. Children are not free to grow and develop their potential without the inner assurance that their parents will remain true in spite of the children's failures and frustrations. And the anxiety rooted deeply in the experience of neurotic individuals will not be touched and overcome until they experience a consistent, secure, and dependable relationship with a parent substitute.

In theology sanctification is considered a threefold process (Thiessen, 1949) in which a person is gradually changed into full maturity. This process begins as a positional event in which God attributes (on the basis of Christ's life and death) holiness to a person who accepts the grace of God. It continues as a process of increasing maturity throughout life. And it culminates in a final and complete perfecting in the eternal state. As an inclusive term embracing the entire process of growth, the doctrine of sanctification can be seen to have major implications for our understanding of human growth and development. Everything Scripture has to say about growth, maturity, and development can be studied for the light it sheds on the conditions, parameters, and means of human growth (see Carter [1974]).

When considering the relationship of the biblical concepts of salvation and sanctification to personality growth and development, a number of crucial questions come to mind. These include:

1. To what extent are biblical teachings on personal growth and maturity simply statements of universal natural principles of growth, and to what extent are they unique to those in the family of God?
2. Are there demonstrable personality changes accompanying the experience of regeneration and conversion?
3. Does the acceptance of human finiteness and sinfulness at the time of salvation generalize to other relationships and settings and enable Christians to more effectively come to grips with their human limitations and consequently increase their level of self-acceptance?
4. Does empirical research support the assumption that the experience of forgiveness that comes at salvation reduces the intensity of personal guilt?
5. If Christian conversion is found not to significantly assist in the resolution of guilt in some individuals, what are the cultural, familial, or intrapersonal factors that prohibit this?
6. Has the church generally carried out the implications of scriptural teachings on sanctification in the relationships and motivations it propounds in its teaching and preaching? What are the consequences of this?
7. How can our psychological understanding of the process of personality development inform our understanding of the biblical concept of sanctification?

Christology and Pneumatology / Counseling

Both therapeutic psychology and Christian theology have a great deal to say about the characteristics of effective helpers. Scripturally, the person and work of both Christ (Christology)[3] and the Holy Spirit (pneumatology) provide divine examples of the central ingredients in an effective helping process.

The doctrines of the Incarnation (God becoming flesh in the person of Jesus Christ) and kenosis (the emptying or humiliation of Christ) speak of Christ's complete identification with humanity. Scripture tells us that Jesus was touched with the feelings of our infirmities (Heb. 4:15). God did not sit idly by and merely observe or reflect over the painful condition of humanity. He stepped into history, took human form, and suffered the limitations of true humanity. In doing so, He once and for all modeled the deep identification so essential in every healing relationship. No better example of personal identification can be found than Christ, who, though He was the Son of God, took on the form of human flesh and suffered all the temptation known to humanity (Heb. 4:15).

But there is another lesson in Christ's coming to humanity. The doctrine of Christ's two natures and the hypostatic union of these two natures in one also has parallels in the therapeutic relationship. While deeply identifying with the hurt and painful perceptions of a counselee, the effective therapist must also maintain another perspective—if you will—a higher perspective. Without removing oneself and losing the ability to empathize and identify, the therapist must bring something more to the relationship. This must be done, however, as a whole person—neither becoming lost in the entanglements of another's struggles nor distancing oneself and losing the empathic sensitivity.

---

[3]Christology can also be looked to in the development of a biblical anthropology. Since humanity is fallen, we will never find our true nature unless we look beyond fallen humanity. Jesus provides this possibility. Unfortunately Evangelicals have often avoided this type of study because of the tendency of Liberals to deny Christ's deity as they emphasize His life as the "ideal man." There are at least five areas of the person of Christ that could be considered in developing a biblical anthropology: (a) Jesus' concept of Himself, (b) His relationships, (c) His volition, (d) His knowledge, and (e) His emotions.

Theologians frequently refer to the "offices of Christ." By this they mean that Scripture sometimes portrays Christ as prophet, sometimes as priest, and sometimes as king. As prophet, Christ confronts humanity with truth. As priest, He is our spokesman, our representative, and our intermediary. He provides the basis for our acceptance. And as king, He superintends. Each of these functions has its parallel in the counselor who sometimes confronts and gives insight (prophetic role), who consistently offers acceptance (priestly role), and who (in one way or another) superintends the counseling process. Carlson (1976) has written on these similarities between the prophetic and priestly aspects of Christ's ministry and the counseling process.

While Christ's propitiation and atonement for sin have no earthly parallel by the very nature of their divine perfection, we can certainly look at the counselor as an agent of reconciliation. It is Christian counselors who have the high privilege of becoming partners in reconciling people to God and consequently to themselves and others.

And just as we can gain insight into effective helping relationships by a study of Christ's life, we can also profit from a study of the person and work of the Holy Spirit. Described as the Paraclete (John 14:16, 26; 15:26; 16:7), the Spirit is our Helper or Comforter. He is the one who comes to our side to help and console. A study of His ministry and person will certainly shed light on the person and role of the human counselor.

Here are a few questions that force themselves to our attention as we consider the implications of our understanding of Christ's life and work for our understanding of the role of the counselor:

1. To what degree (if any) can we look at Christ's relationships with others as a model for therapeutic counseling? In other words, is there justification in studying the life of Christ in our search for the development of a counseling model?
2. Are some aspects of Christ's life and ministry more relevant to counseling and the personality and role of the therapist than others?

3. What are the implications for the counselor of Christ's threefold role as prophet, priest, and king?
4. The Holy Spirit is called the Counselor. To what extent is His ministry to us a model for the counselor?
5. Why do some Christians need (or seem to need) a counselor if the Holy Spirit is the Counselor?
6. How can the Christian counselor develop Christlike attitudes in order to be a more effective helper?

Ecclesiology / Social Psychology

Both Scripture and social psychology address numerous issues that have to do with the relationships between individuals and within groups. Theologically, biblical revelations on interpersonal processes are generally discussed under the heading of ecclesiology (doctrine of the church). While the doctrine of the church includes much more than counsel on relationships (e.g., the mission and ordinances of the church), it does contain a great deal that has a broad application to the whole field of social psychology in general and group processes in particular.

The New Testament stresses three concepts that are especially significant here: ecclesia, koinonia, and agape. *Ecclesia* emphasizes the idea of a called-out people joining together—that is, it speaks of a group comprised of individual personalities with a common bond; *koinonia* emphasizes the idea of fellowship or sharing; and *agape* speaks of a deep and unconditional love for other persons as they are. According to Scripture, the dynamics of these three concepts provide a cornerstone for the maturing of the members of the body of Christ. It is within the context of the church as a body of believers that Scripture discusses personal growth.

> It was he who gave some to be apostles, some to be prophets, some to be evangelists, and some to be pastors and teachers, to prepare God's people for works of service, so that the body of Christ may be built up until we reach unity in the faith and in the knowledge of the Son of God and become mature, attaining to the whole measure of the fullness of Christ. Then we will no longer be infants, tossed back and forth by the waves, and blown here and there by every wind of teaching and by the cunning and craftiness

of men in their deceitful scheming. Instead, speaking the truth in love, we will in all things grow up into him who is the Head, that is, Christ. From him the whole body, joined and held together by every supporting ligament, grows and builds itself up in love, as each part does its work. (Eph. 4:11-16)

During the last decade or two, the Christian church has begun to address the role of interpersonal relations in the growth and maturity of members of the church community. Books by Keith Miller (1965), Ray Stedman (1972), and Ray Ortlund (1974) have all spoken to the oft-neglected truth that Christians cannot mature simply through an intellectual understanding of biblical revelation.

Students of psychology should readily see the similarity between many scriptural principles of interpersonal relations and the dynamics found in every therapeutic group experience. While the goals, composition, and leadership techniques may vary, both the "body life" movement and the group movement within psychology are focusing on similar dynamics. Acceptance, commitment, caring, confrontation, encouragement, responsibility, and security are all interpersonal issues that Scripture clearly addresses within the context of the church as the "body of Christ." In fact, one suspects that if the church had been operating on the basis of a scriptural model of interpersonal relating, it would have been a much more effective healing agent than has been the case.

In addition to the more obviously biblical principles of relating, many social-psychological concepts appear to have real value in studying and clarifying the dynamics of relationships within the church and in better understanding church growth and related issues. When attempting to relate the scriptural teachings to social psychology and therapy groups, several critical questions come to mind.

1. What is the biblical pattern for growth-producing, personal relationships and how does this relate to current social-psychological thinking?

2. How does current social-psychological research on leadership relate to scriptural concepts of leadership and to biblical examples of leadership such as Moses, Joshua, and David?

3. How does research on interpersonal attraction and friendship relate to the commandment that Christians are not to be respecters of persons?
4. How does the biblical model of church government and the concept of spiritual gifts relate to the principles of organizational structure, organizational function, and social roles?
5. If Scripture portrays the church as a caring, accepting community, why are so many looking outside the church for growth groups and similar experiences?
6. Why has the church frequently been reticent to confront and discipline its members?

Eschatology / Psychology of Motivation

Eschatology refers to the Bible's teachings regarding the last judgment, the second coming of Christ, and the end time. In these events human history, as we know it, ends and those who have been reconciled to God through Christ begin their fellowship with Him in eternity. The psychology of motivation encompasses a study of all of the forces, drives, and reasons for human behavior. In this section we are going to focus on only one aspect of motivation, that of rewards, goals, and expectations.

The differences between biblical eschatology and the psychology of rewards, expectations, and goals seems obvious. The latter describes events that are much less cosmic and much more finite in nature. There are, however, some areas of overlap. To begin with, all human living involves goal setting and goal seeking. There are no purely purposeless human actions. While psychologists have not, as a rule, discussed purpose, the concept of motivation certainly implies this concept. Self-actualization, for example, implies purpose as an end state. Thus, a great deal of what the actualization theorists (e.g., Rogers, 1951; Maslow, 1970) have described as maturity and/or a fully functioning person becomes a goal. Thus while human history moves toward its final goal or end, so human behavior repeatedly moves toward specific or more limited goals.

Similarly, both theology and psychology speak of hope. The Bible describes the second coming of Christ as the blessed hope of the Christian. While there have been only a few systematic psychological investigations of hope (Mowrer, 1961; Stotland, 1969; Tolman, 1958), psychology, especially existential psychology, has extensively described fear, anxiety, and despair—concepts that are the reverse of hope.

A third integrative aspect of eschatology is the concept of judgment. Judgment (either human or divine) means reward and punishment that is based on personal responsibility. Psychologists have thoroughly discussed the concepts of rewards, punishments, and incentives. Scripture, too, speaks of rewards and punishments, both in terms of the immediate rewards of holy living and in terms of the final judgment of the wicked and the rewarding of the righteous. In spite of the vast differences between the ultimate end of humanity as described in Scripture and the concerns of psychology, it seems that at least in the areas of goal setting, hope, and rewards, we have psychological phenomena that are integrable with their cosmic eschatological equivalents. Here are other questions that surface in considering the relationship between biblical eschatology and the psychology of rewards, expectations, and goals:

1. How are we to understand the motives for reward (theologically), and what are the implications of this for a theory of motivation?
2. What is the role of hope in both human motivation and emotional adjustment?
3. In what ways does the biblical concept of the second coming of Christ as the Christian's "blessed hope" relate to personal adjustment in general and optimism in particular?
4. What implications does the biblical concept of reward and punishment have for the process of child rearing and discipline?
5. Can the Christian understanding of future full development in eternity be utilized as a vision of possibilities for persons living on earth, thus serving as a positive motivation for growth?
6. How does the psychological concept of responsibility and choice relate to the biblical concept of accountability?

SUMMARY   This concludes our brief survey of the possibilities of integrating our understanding of the major doctrines of systematic theology with the major considerations of psychology. We have not attempted to elaborate on all of the integrative possibilities; we have merely suggested the potential richness of an integrative study and outlined one possible structure for approaching the task of integration.

Much the same approach could be taken to a study of moral theology (Christian ethics), practical theology, and Christian education. For example, how should we relate scriptural teachings on morality to the research and theory of psychologists such as Kohlberg (1964) and Piaget (1948)? What do they have to contribute to our understanding of moral development? And what can Christian educators learn from educational psychologists that will speed up the assimilation of biblical teaching and ensure its lasting impact on students in church educational programs? Every branch of theology addresses issues of concern to psychology, and much is to be gained by a continuing dialogue and an effort to find common ground, unifying principles, and broadened understandings. This makes the scope of possibilities for the integration of psychology and theology very wide indeed!

THE
AGAINST MODEL

In the brief one-hundred-year **4** history of psychology, there have been numerous at- tempts to relate the facts and theories of psychology to the affirmations of theology. These attempts run the gamut from outright rejection of the notion of integrating two such separate disciplines to some very sophisti- cated attempts to find common ground and integrable concepts in the statements of psychologists and theologians.

In this and the next three chapters we will attempt to order these diverse approaches and demonstrate how each can be located in one of four general approaches to, or models of, integration. By looking at the presuppositions and perspectives held in common by theorists within each model we can begin to see both the potential and the problems of various approaches to the relationship of psychology and theology. In each chapter we will briefly outline one of the four models of integration and state its basic premises and hypotheses. Then we will illustrate the perspective of that model by citing several representative authors and conclude with a brief summary.

In this way we will attempt to demonstrate how the representatives of each viewpoint approach issues such as the nature and sources of truth, the nature of religious and psychological data, and the possibility of relating these two types of data. It is our belief that some of these approaches are doomed to failure. They can never effect a viable integration because of their built-in presuppositions. Others hold more promise.

In outlining each model, we will present both a secular and a sacred version.[1] Since these versions have developed separately, there will be some difference in terminology. Psychologists with an interest in religion have generally been concerned with broad religious phenomena and experience, and, as a result, they have explored the relationship between psychology and religion in general. In contrast, the Christian authors we will discuss generally represent orthodox Christian viewpoints. They have been more concerned with theology and with the nature and effects of Christianity than with religion in general. In spite of these differences, however, it appears to us that there is sufficient similarity in underlying presuppositions to consider the sacred and secular version of each model as two sides of the same coin.

We have chosen to call these models the Against model, the Of model, the Parallels model, and the Integrates model.[2] We will begin our discussion with the *Against* model. Although this model represents an extreme viewpoint that is antithetical to the tenets of this book, it does serve as a good reference point from which we can build a comprehensive understanding of the relationship between psychology and theology.

---

[1] In using the terms *secular* and *sacred* we are not implying a division of truth into two spheres nor a lack of commitment to the unity of all truth under God. We are instead referring to the fact that theoretical approaches can be loosely categorized into those that take into consideration the existence of God and divine revelation and those that do not.

[2] Our thinking on models for the integration of psychology and theology follows in a general way H. Richard Niebuhr's analysis of the history of relations between Christianity and civilization as outlined in *Christ and Culture* (New York: Harper and Row, 1951).

THE AGAINST MODEL The Against model is built on the as-
(SECULAR VERSION) sumption that there are inherent conflicts
between psychology and religion on the
one hand and between Christianity and psychology on the other.
For a variety of reasons holders of this view maintain that psychology and Christianity are essentially incompatible and that there is
no real possibility for integration. In fact, proponents of this model
frequently set psychology and theology against each other in ways
that suggest that they are mortal enemies.

Epistemology

The secular version of the Against model begins with the assumption that rationalism and empiricism are the only valid means to
truth and that the truth claims of revealed religions are necessarily in
conflict with the findings and methods of the science of psychology.
Because psychology and religion hold conflicting views of epistemology, representatives of this viewpoint assume that there will
be numerous conflicts in the "findings" of the two disciplines. They
also assume that since psychology and religion are built upon
different views of knowledge, there can be no way of arbitrating or
reconciling these conflicting viewpoints. In fact, the attempt to arrive at an understanding of the human personality from any viewpoint other than that of scientific psychology is viewed as a step
back to the inadequate and nonscientific thinking of the past. Religion is at best allowable for children and primitives. At its worst it
perpetuates immaturity and irrationality.

One of the best-known secular proponents of the Against
model is Albert Ellis. In a paper entitled "The Psychotherapist's Case
Against Religion" (Note 3), Ellis laid down his view that religion and
science are incompatible.

In regard to scientific thinking it practically goes without saying
that this kind of cerebration is quite antithetical to religiosity. The
main canon of the scientific method is that at least in some final
analysis or in principle all theories must be confirmable by some
form of human experience—some empirical referent. It could
well be contended that the more religious one is the less scientific
one tends to be. Although a religious person need not be entirely

unscientific, as for that matter a raving maniac need not be either, it is difficult to see how he could be perfectly scientific. And while a person may be both scientific and religious, as he may also be at times sensible and at times foolish, it is doubtful whether his attitude may simultaneously be truly pious and objective.

Here we have a clear presentation of the epistemological viewpoint in the secular Against model. Science is the only source of truth, and religion is antithetical to scientific thinking.

Religion and Mental Health

A second characteristic of the secular Against model is the belief that religion has a negative effect on mental health. Typically, representatives of the secular Against model see religion as destructive of emotional balance. In the paper cited above Ellis makes the following statements:

> If religion is defined as man's dependence on a power above and beyond the human then as a psychotherapist I find it to be exceptionally pernicious.

> In most respects religion seriously sabotages mental health.

> The very essence of most organized religions is the performance of masochistic, guilt soothing rituals by which the religious individual gives himself permission to enjoy life. Religiosity to a large degree essentially then is masochism and both are forms of mental sickness.

Ellis also maintains that religion promotes dependency, inflexibility, rigidity, and bigotry. Although Ellis's viewpoint is extreme, he is by no means alone. Ralph Greenson, author of a widely used textbook on psychoanalysis (1967), makes the following comments in a taped lecture entitled "The Conflict Between Religion and Psychoanalysis" (n.d.):

> Faith and obedience impair the intellectual development of men.

> Worship of anything makes you the worshiper insignificant. The greater God is, the lowlier is the worshiper.

> By elevating anything to godlike proportions, you degrade the worshiper.

In a similar view, Eli Chesen (1972) complains that religion inhibits individuals and society and that it induces rigidity and unfounded, neurotic guilt. Here are a few of his comments:

> Suffice it to say that it [religion] seldom provides a major positive influence on the normal process of emotional development that, it is hoped, leads to mental health. In most cases it has not done so and cannot, for it is too rigid and can never change rapidly enough. Though religion may at one time have served man, man is now serving religion, and often at his own expense. . . . Religion demands service by dictating rules to be followed and sacrifices to be made, but often gives very little to its followers in return. (p. 26)

> The concept of hell is also useless and harmful. I suspect that those evangelists who continue to peddle this asinine idea are beyond redemption. Inculcation with such a negative entity as hell makes for intriguing books and horror movies, but does little to promote a healthy attitude toward religion. (p. 93)

> From my experience, I tend to look with a jaundiced eye at the more fundamental and/or evangelical Protestant faiths, and I directly question the conscious motives of many of their clergymen. They seem to preach the most hazardous brand of religion, and for this reason I would start any checklist by rating these religious movements at the bottom. (pp. 125-126)

Psychopathology and Therapy

A third assumption of the secular Against model has to do with the origin and resolution of psychological disturbances. Operating from naturalistic assumptions, the secular Against psychologist assumes that personal maladjustments result from social or psychological causes and that the solution to these difficulties will be found only in some form of psychological or sociological treatment. Since there are no spiritual sources of psychological disturbances, there are no spiritual solutions. In fact, one of the therapist's tasks may be to rid patients of the neurotic effects of belief in God. Ellis (Note 3) states:

> So will the therapist, if he himself is not too sick or gutless, attack his patient's religiosity. Not only will he show his patient that he is religious . . . the therapist will also quite vigorously and forcefully question, challenge, and attack the patient's emotional beliefs that support these disturbed traits.

Needless to say, opinions such as those of Ellis, Chesen, and Greenson have done little to endear psychology to the hearts of pastors, theologians, or Christians in general. Instead, they erect barriers and allow no common ground for the search for truth. But while such antagonistic viewpoints seem extreme, they are by no means limited to secular psychologists. The religious version of the Against model is often held with equal fervor and rigidity. In fact, in some Christian quarters a staunch Against attitude toward psychology is held out as evidence of one's fidelity to Scripture.

THE AGAINST MODEL (SACRED VERSION) The Christian version of the Against model has striking parallels to the secular viewpoint. From the beginning, proponents of this perspective set psychology over against Christianity. The possibility of mutual cooperation is not even considered a worthwhile option. Billheimer (1977) seems to rule out the possibility of integration when he states: "While there are professing Christian psychiatrists, it seems a misnomer to this writer" (p. 94).

Epistemology

Like the secular Against view, proponents of this perspective also claim to have a corner on the truth. In this instance the sole source of truth is revelation rather than reason or scientific investigation. Solomon (1971), for example, writes:

> Persons representing every discipline (and no discipline) are forwarding theories about human behavior in futile attempts to bring order out of chaos. Various behavioristic approaches proffered by both the secular and religious communities aim to lead individuals and groups to tranquillity and fulfillment. Most of these approaches require great outlays of capital and depend solely on human resources for their implementation. Since most of these are based on the temporal, rather than the eternal, the results will be ephemeral, if not a total waste of time. (p. 17)

Although Christian proponents of the Against model may give passing assent to the validity of reason and empirical evidence, much of their writing calls into question both the data and the theories of modern psychology. Jay Adams (1970) writes:

The conclusions in this book are not based upon scientific findings. My method is presuppositional. I avowedly accept the inerrant Bible as the standard of all faith and practice. The Scriptures, therefore, are the basis, and contain the criteria by which I have sought to make every judgment. . . . I do not wish to disregard science, but rather I welcome it as a useful adjunct for the purposes of illustrating, filling in generalizations with specifics, and challenging wrong human interpretations of Scripture, thereby, forcing the student to restudy the Scriptures. However, in the area of psychology, science has largely given way to humanistic philosophy and gross speculation. (p. xx)

Adams does give a perfunctory nod to the scientific method, but he concludes that there is very little of science in psychology. This quotation, as well as the comments of Solomon, reflect the tendency within this Against model to set psychology against Scripture.

Psychology and Mental Health

Christians operating from an Against view not only hold firmly to their belief in one source of truth, they also see other truth claims and their working out in therapy and society as potentially dangerous to mental and emotional health. Just as secular Against authors are concerned with the potentially negative effects of religion on a person's psyche, so Christian Against authors are concerned about the possible negative influence of psychology. In fact, both sides frequently accuse one another of negatively influencing both people's external behavior and their guilt emotions. Only the concerns are reversed. Whereas secular Against authors fear that religion will inhibit people and promote excessive guilt, Christian Against authors see psychology as breaking down needed inhibitions and removing valid guilt.

Psychopathology and Therapy

When we come to therapy, we find this approach carried to its logical conclusion. Since personal maladjustment results from sin, there is no need for psychotherapy. What is needed is spiritual counsel or advice.

Adams (1970), commenting on his contacts with psychiatric patients during a one-summer training program, draws the following conclusion:

> Apart from those who had organic problems, like brain damage, the people I met in the two institutions in Illinois were there because of their own failure to meet life's problems. To put it simply, they were there because of their unforgiven and unaltered sinful behavior. (p. xvi)

And Solomon (1971) states:

> Psychotherapy, then, has as its goal to help a person become stronger and stronger. But God says we must become weaker and weaker that He might become our strength. . . . Thus psychotherapy is at cross purposes with God and becomes a substitute for the work of the Holy Spirit. (p. 27)

> This is not to say that a Christian who does therapy is insincere either in his therapy or in his relationship with the Lord Jesus Christ; it is to say that he either has not experienced the abundant life or he doesn't know how to share it in a clinical setting. If he did, he would be forced to repudiate most of his techniques as being of questionable value at best and cease *his* therapy in deference to the Holy Spirit's. (pp. 32-33)

By now a pattern should be apparent. At almost every point the Christian Against theorist takes an attitude toward the interface of psychology and Christianity that is almost identical to that of the secular Against theorists. The attitude, the perspectives, and the presuppositions are almost identical. Only the content is reversed, with the Christian taking an opposite stance to the secular theorist on every issue.

SUMMARY AND EVALUATION

Table 4 summarizes the major assumptions of those holding an Against view of psychology and theology. The assumptions on the left are found in the secular realm, and those on the right issue out of a Christian context. This summary will serve as the basis for a brief evaluation of the strengths and weaknesses of this model.

TABLE 4—THE AGAINST MODEL

SECULAR	SACRED
• There is only one reliable means of finding truth (the scientific method with its use of rationalism and empiricism).	• There is only one reliable means of finding truth (revelation).
• Other truth claims (revelation) are potentially destructive.	• Other truth claims (rationalism and empiricism) are potentially destructive.
• Religion's potential destructiveness relates especially to inhibitions and guilt. (It causes inhibitions and guilt.)	• Psychology's potential destructiveness relates especially to inhibitions and guilt. (It removes inhibitions and rationalizes guilt.)
• Personal maladjustments are rooted in one basic cause (psychological).	• Personal maladjustments are rooted in one basic cause (spiritual).
• The solution to personal maladjustments is found in one dimension (psychological).	• The solution to personal maladjustments is found in one dimension (spiritual).

By way of evaluation, we see no advantages to the Against model. Although some may think that the rhetoric of the secular and sacred camps serves to balance each other's perspective, the truth is that they rarely, if ever, listen to one another. The oppositional stance inherent in both of these views does not allow proponents to step out of their own perspective to understand the suppositions, methodology, and reasoning of those holding other views. The Against model is a rigid, defensive way of looking at things that does not allow for stimulation, clarification, and integration.

A second disadvantage of the Against model is its limited epistemology. Secular proponents see no place for revelation and Christian proponents see little place for general revelation and common grace. Both of these perspectives run counter to the traditional orthodox commitment to the fact that God is the author of all truth and that truth is found through both the inspired Word and the study of creation.

A final weakness of the Against model is found especially in the

Christian version. Although it is not a necessary corollary of the sacred Against model, it seems that most proponents of this model hold a relatively superficial view of sin. Perhaps in reaction against the emphasis on the unconscious, the inner life, and the influence of the past among dynamically oriented psychologists, sacred Against theorists tend to reduce sin (or psychopathology) to either observable actions and attitudes or to specific behavioral symptoms. Although theologically they may know better, their writings imply that a person's problems can generally be traced to doing, saying, or thinking the wrong things. Thus therapy essentially becomes telling the counselee what the Bible says and how he or she should respond. Biblical emphases on the attitudes of the heart (Ps. 51:6; Matt. 12:34-35) and of the impact of parents and a sinful society on a person's adjustment are minimized in favor of behavioral compliance and a narrow view of personal responsibility.

These weaknesses lead us to make one final observation about the sacred Against model. The proponents of this model tend to rely extensively on scriptural data that is selectively incorporated into their model. At first glance proponents of the Against model often seem to have wrestled with biblical issues. But a word of caution is in order. The sheer volume of biblical references may be a poor guide to the adequacy of any theoretical perspective.

None of us approach Scripture without built-in biases and perceptions. Yet because proponents of the Against model hold a limited view of epistemology and are generally better trained in theology than they are in either philosophy or psychology, they often seem unaware of this personal factor. In sincerely attempting to build a Christian theory of personality or counseling they can, in a sense, be more susceptible to error than those who are more acutely aware of their own finiteness. Awareness of our human frailty and personal biases tends to bring a humility that is less prone to *have* answers and is more inclined to be open to the findings, perspectives, and understandings of our colleagues.

THE
OF MODEL

We call the second approach **5** to the relationship of psychology and Christianity the Of model. In this model there is an attempt to find "good" psychology in religion or to find the psychology *of* religion. Rather than seeing irreconcilable differences between the two realms, as is the case among those who hold the Against model, proponents of the Of view maintain that there is a great deal of common ground between psychology and religion that should be explored.

Working from humanistic, mystical, and/or naturalistic assumptions, both secular and sacred proponents of this view see the person as a spiritual-moral being (in the broad, humanistic sense of the term). For them any technology, religion, science, or society that denies the human being's inner spirit, and consequently the person's true nature, is suspect. Since both good psychology and good religion stress the importance of this uniquely human-spiritual quality, psychology and religion have a great deal in common and can be of great benefit to one another when there is open exchange between the two realms.

THE OF MODEL (SECULAR VERSION) The secular Of model minimizes the purely religious nature or content of religious concepts and rejects any supernaturalism. The elements of religion that are viewed as helpful (and consequently relatable to psychology) are the metaphors used to express universal human experience and truth. In this model, scriptural revelation about events such as the Fall are stripped of both their supernatural element and their historical reality and are interpreted instead as expressions of humanity's universal struggle to be truly human and to rise above the shackles of inner bondage. Scripture is infused with a particular psychological meaning or theory, and consequently it becomes a vehicle for the expression of psychological truth.

In viewing the Bible as a book of good psychology, the Of model's adherents typically distinguish between healthy and unhealthy religions. Healthy religions are broadly humanistic. They promote loving sensitivity to oneself and others. Unhealthy religions are the more conservative ones, especially those with an authoritarian structure, and those that take concepts of sin, guilt, and hell literally.

Eric Fromm is a good representative of this perspective. In the Foreword to *Psychoanalysis and Religion* (1950) Fromm clearly sets off his approach from practicing religionists and from practicing analysts.

> If I undertake to discuss the problem of religion and psychoanalysis afresh in these chapters it is because I want to show that to set up alternatives of either irreconcilable opposition or identity of interest is fallacious; a thorough and dispassionate discussion can demonstrate that the relation between religion and psychoanalysis is too complex to be forced into either one of these simple and convenient attitudes. (p. 9)

As a nontheistic humanist, Fromm can accept neither of these views; so he attempts instead to find some mutuality of interest or some common ground between religion and psychoanalysis (Fromm, 1950).

I want to show in these pages that it is not true that we have to give up the concern for the soul if we do not accept the tenets of religion. The psychoanalyst is in a position to study the human reality behind religion as well as behind nonreligious symbol systems. He finds that the question is not whether man returns to religion and believes in God but whether he lives love and thinks truth. If he does so the symbol systems he uses are of secondary importance. If he does not they are of no importance. (p. 9)

When Fromm refers to the "symbols" of religion, he is not speaking of belief in God or the Bible. He is saying that religion is useful to the degree that it helps a person live more fully. The unique nature and supernatural aspects of the Bible are passed over or mythologized. The Bible becomes a book of psychology.

Fromm (1950) goes on to describe more fully the common humanistic goal of psychoanalysis and religion:

In trying to give a picture of the human attitude underlying the thinking of Lao-tse, Buddha, the Prophets, Socrates, Jesus, Spinoza, and the philosophers of the Enlightenment, one is struck by the fact that in spite of significant differences there is a core of ideas and norms common to all of these teachings. Without attempting to arrive at a complete and precise formulation, the following is an approximate description of this common core: man must strive to recognize the truth and can be fully human only to the extent to which he succeeds in this task. He must be independent and free, an end in himself and not the means for any other person's purposes. He must relate himself to his fellow man lovingly. If he has no love, he is an empty shell even if his were all power, wealth, and intelligence. Man must know the difference between good and evil, he must learn to listen to the voice of his conscience and be able to follow it.

[So I] attempt to show that the aim of the psychoanalytic cure of the soul is to help the patient attain the attitude which I just described as religious. (pp. 73-74)

So, according to Fromm, religion is constructive (and congruent with psychoanalysis) to the degree that it promotes freedom, love, truth, and independence. One religion is no better than another because all great religious teachers were propounding a quite similar view of the good life.

From an entirely different theoretical perspective, Mowrer (1961) also demonstrates an Of perspective.

By who

> Sin used to be—and, in some quarters, still is—defined as what-ever one does that puts him in danger of going to Hell. Here was an assumed cause-and-effect relationship that was completely metaphysical and empirically unverifiable; and it is small wonder that it has fallen into disrepute as the scientific outlook and method have steadily gained in acceptance and manifest power. But there is a very tangible and very present Hell-on-this-earth which science has not yet helped us understand very well; and so I invite your attention to the neglected but very real possibility that it is this Hell—the Hell of neurosis and psychosis—to which sin and unexpiated guilt lead us and that it is this Hell that gives us one of the most, perhaps the most realistic and basic criteria for defining sin and guilt. If it proves empirically true that certain forms of conduct characteristically lead human beings into emotional instability, what better or firmer basis would one wish for labeling such conduct as destructive, self-defeating, evil, sinful? (p. 42)

And Karl Menninger (1975), in his widely read *Whatever Became of Sin?*, explains that when he uses the word *sin* he means

> any kind of wrongdoing that we used to call sin. I have in mind behavior that violates the moral code or the individual conscience or both; behavior which pains or harms or destroys my neighbor—or me, myself. (pp. 17-18)

The redefinition of sin by Mowrer and Menninger is typical of proponents of an Of model. The supernatural and revelational aspects of Scripture are rejected in favor of an approach that looks for the psychology *of* Scripture. Sin is no longer an offense against a personal God and hell is no longer the eternal abode of the wicked. Hell is the hell of neurosis and psychosis, and sin is whatever sends you there. Christianity's emphasis on morality and responsibility is good to the degree that we empirically find that certain behavior leads to neurotic or psychotic maladjustments. And for Menninger sin is a good word to describe our moral violations. But it refers more to violations of human relationships than it does to rebellion against God.

THE OF MODEL   The Christian version of the Of model is
(SACRED VERSION)   very similar to the secular version because
its proponents have generally come from
theologically liberal traditions that, like their secular counterparts,
reject the supernatural elements of Christianity and take a strongly
humanistic and/or naturalistic attitude toward religion. Although
proponents of this model may (like holders of the sacred Against
model) maintain a careful distinction between the Bible and the
facts of science and reason, they tend to elevate the claims of science and reason to a place above the authority of Scripture.

Proponents of the sacred version of the Of model stress the
universal aspects of the Bible rather than the supernatural and redemptive aspects. They focus on love, freedom, responsibility, and
similar virtues but gloss over or redefine the Bible's emphasis on sin
and the need for personal salvation. These concepts are an offense
and are not seen as necessary for a proper understanding of the
human being. A God of creation or providence is acceptable but not
a God of justice and redemption. Christianity is not viewed as essentially different from other religions. Its symbols may be different
and Christ is viewed as the "ultimate man," but at its core Christianity is simply another way to the truth of the good life.

Another characteristic of the Christian Of model is its attempt
to interpret the tenets of various schools of psychology as truly
redemptive and Christian. Proponents of this view *selectively*
translate or interpret various passages or concepts from the Bible for
use in their particular psychology. Certain aspects of the Bible are
mapped into the writings of some school of psychology or translated
into a particular theoretical system. The founder of the theory, be he
Freud, Jung, or Rogers, becomes elevated so that what is acceptable
in the Bible is what fits into the particular theory. Thus, the view to
be propagated and used as a therapeutic tool is the Christianized
version of some psychological theorist.

This translating of scriptural data into a psychological theory
differs from the attempts to relate the Bible to a particular theory of
psychology (the Parallels model) described in the next chapter. In
the Parallels model Scripture is seen as having two levels of mean-

ing or interpretation. One is distinctly spiritual and supernatural. The other is psychological. Both are seen as valid. In the Of model this parallel does not exist. The *true* meaning of Scripture is found in its psychology. This perspective *replaces* traditional scriptural understandings instead of adding to them.

Note that the traditional Christian understanding of both the concept of God and several Scripture passages are replaced by a radically different interpretation in the following quotation from a book by James and Savary (1974) dealing with transactional analysis and religious experience.

> The energy channeled to the three ego states by the Inner Core is a positive personal force—a power for good and growth. We term the force the Power Within. Others may prefer to call the source of this inner power God, Spirit, Nature, Ground of Being or some other name. Paul the Apostle was referring to this Power Within when he asked, "Do you know that God's Spirit dwells in you?" To describe the Power Within, Jesus used the water-of-life symbol. "If anyone thirsts," he said, "let him come to me and drink." As Scripture says, from within him will flow rivers of living water. . . . People never need to run out of this inner power since its source is the divine power creatively pulsing deep down within everything in the universe. (p. 20)

Many attempts at relating psychology and theology from a liberal theological perspective have taken an Of position, and we will cite two more examples. First a quotation from John Sanford (1968), an Episcopal priest trained in Jungian psychology.

> When we grasp that the psyche contains this energy-filled image of God we begin to understand why the men of the Bible and of the early Church felt dreams to be expressions of the Deity. For our dreams express these psychic inner energies; they relate us to the center of these energies, and they place us in contact with a kind of unconscious direction which these energies serve. In short, our dreams express the Mind of God within us. This understanding also leads us to a comprehension of certain things in the development of religion, and to further interesting comparisons between psychology and traditional Christian theological formulations. (p. 204)

Although Sanford earlier stresses the importance of making "a careful semantic distinction between God as Ultimate Reality and the self, or inner image of God, existing in our psyche," it becomes clear that his understanding of God differs significantly from the orthodox Christian view. Although the conception of God here may not be Tillich's "Ultimate Concern," in Sanford's thinking God is certainly in some way a projection of our inner self. The author goes on to explain polytheism as the projection of our disunity outward, while monotheism results not from the objective reality of God as one but from the projection of a more unified personal center outward.

Another author whose writings often reflect an Of perspective is Seward Hiltner. In *Theological Dynamics* (1972) he writes:

> To assert that sin has an "original" or given dimension means that, over and above whatever freedom the person had that he misused, there are social and historical forces at work within the man and within society that require repentance and constructive change. It was clear to the ancients as it is to us today that many of man's acts are conditioned by social and historical forces in the face of which he is partially bound. This fact is acknowledged by understanding sin to have an "original" aspect or dimension. Such a conviction helps to prevent the idea of sin from degenerating into blame, especially blame of the individual person. (p. 83)

In an attempt to relate theological and psychological concepts, Hiltner rejects the orthodox understanding of original sin and substitutes an environmental view that fits more neatly with his psychological beliefs.[1] Original sin becomes the conditioning processes of society rather than the effects of Adam and Eve's sin transmitted personally to every human being. While we would certainly agree that sin has a social dimension and that frequently we are as much sinned against as we are sinful, Hiltner's analysis reinterprets Scripture for the purpose of fitting it into his psychological system. Although his writings contain many penetrating insights, his treatment of the Bible makes it a Scripture *of* psychology.

---

[1] In so doing he reflects an essentially Pelagian view of human nature.

Here we see the basic similarity of the sacred and secular Of models. Although the sacred version originates within a religious context and its proponents possess a personal religious identity, the assumptions and content of the model are not significantly different from the secular version.

SUMMARY AND EVALUATION

Table 5 summarizes the essential assumptions and attitudes of those holding the Of model.

TABLE 5—THE OF MODEL

SECULAR	SACRED
• Basic epistemology: Pantheism, humanism, or naturalism that is broader than a reductionistic naturalism.	• Basic epistemology: Pantheism, humanism, or naturalism that is broader than a reductionistic naturalism. Scripture and religious experiences are valid sources of truth but not in a clearly supernatural way.
• Nature of the Human Being: Each person is a spiritual-moral being in at least a broadly humanistic sense.	• Nature of the Human Being: Each person is a spiritual-moral being.
• Value of religion: Most religions recognize the spiritual-moral nature of the human being and are consequently good.	• Value of religion: The creative, providential, and relational aspects of religion are its core. The supernatural and redemptive elements are useful as symbols but are not to be taken literally.
• A theological definition of sin must be discarded in favor of a truly psychological and/or environmental definition.	• Sin is essentially a religious symbol for psychopathology.
• Psychology and religion: Good psychology translates the valid insights of religion and uses them for human good.	• Religion and psychology: Emotional growth is promoted by the use of psychological principles in a religious setting with religious metaphors.

The Of model, while being a more helpful perspective than the Against model, still has serious limitations—at least for those committed to an orthodox view of Scripture. While it does open the possibility of meaningful dialogue between psychologists and theologians, it does so at the expense of the evangelical view of Scripture. It takes a cookie-cutter approach in which the theories of psychology are pressed onto the dough of Scripture. The dough that fits within the cutter is retained while whatever falls outside is rejected.

This cookie-cutter style is the main weakness of the Of approach. It *reduces* Scripture (or religion) to psychology and robs it of its revelational and supernatural content. Once this is done there is really no ground for integration because the unique contributions of Christianity have been set aside. What is left is simply psychology from the human perspective.

THE
PARALLELS MODEL

We label the third approach **6** to the relation of psychology and Christianity the Parallels model because proponents of this viewpoint treat the con- cepts of psychology and Christianity in ways that parallel each other but rarely truly integrate. Psychology is treated as a valid and necessary science (or profession), and Christianity (or religion) is viewed as a normal (and perhaps helpful) personal or societal phenomenon. Both psychology and Christianity have their rightful place. Psychology is a science, and religion is a personal experience or commitment. Holders of the Parallels view are generally active in both psychology and Christianity and may even have published in both spheres. But there is little if any effort to engage in dialogue that would pose new questions, open new vistas, and in other ways generate an interface between the two disciplines or perspectives.

There are two versions of the parallels model. The first is the isolation version. Holders of this version maintain that psychology and the Scriptures (or theology) are separate and there is little or no significant overlap. That is, each is encapsulated, and there is little interaction because the methods and contents of each discipline are different. Since both are valid, however, both must be affirmed although they remain isolated.

The second version of the Parallels model can be called the correlation version. Holders of this approach attempt to correlate or align certain psychological and scriptural concepts. They may suggest, for example, that the superego is equivalent to the conscience or that the id is equivalent to lust or the flesh or the old nature.

Holders of the correlation version sometimes assume they are integrating when in actuality they are aligning concepts from different spheres. The basic difference between correlating and integrating (which will become clearer after the Integrates model is discussed) is that correlating assumes there are two things that need to be lined up and thus retain the system or configuration of concepts in each; integrating assumes there is ultimately only one set (configuration) of concepts, laws, or principles that operates in two disciplines. Genuine integration involves the discovery and articulation of the common underlying principles of both psychology and the Scriptures. It is this discovery of the one overarching configuration or set of principles that constitutes the deepest level of integration, not simply the lining up of parallel concepts from two distinct disciplines.

The Parallels model is a distinct improvement over the Against and Of models since it preserves the integrity of both psychology and Christianity. And it is probably the position most often taken by thoughtful psychologists who, while not minimizing the importance of either Christianity or psychology, want to be sure to avoid superficial attempts at integration that violate the unity and integrity of either.

THE PARALLELS MODEL (SECULAR VERSION) The secular version of the Parallels model is more difficult to define than its Christian counterpart since few secular psychologists have expressed this kind of thinking in written form. It is probably, however, a view widely held by psychological practitioners. One clear example of this perspective is Frederick Thorne (1950), for many years the editor of the *Journal of Clinical Psychology*. He writes:

> Primary reliance should be placed on scientific methods when they are validly applicable, but . . . philosophy and religion also have their proper sphere of activities beyond the realm of science. (p. 471)
>
> A distinction should be made between religion-oriented spiritual counseling and scientifically oriented personality counseling. . . . It must be recognized in the beginning that the theoretical and philosophical foundations of spiritual and scientific approaches are basically different. (p. 481)

While Thorne goes on to discuss the place of religion in counseling, his isolationist position is clear. Counseling, as scientifically based and grounded, is separate and even at points in opposition to religiously oriented counseling; yet there is clearly a place for religion as part of knowledge and culture. Also, its influence on certain counselees must be recognized and addressed.

Linn and Schwarz (1958) also suggest an isolationist approach. They write:

> The fact that in certain areas psychology and religion border upon each other has made it easy to confuse their respective roles. . . . Developments in psychiatry are no more related to religion than parallel developments in other branches of medicine. (pp. 9, 11)

Again we see the strong desire to segregate religion and psychiatry into their respective domains. Each has a role, but it must be clear that they are strictly parallel and not different aspects of a broader unity.

Gordon Allport is another psychologist whose writings at points reflect an integrated approach but were generally done from a parallel (correlational) perspective. Consider, for example, the following statements (1950):

> In stating this fact the vocabulary of religion and of modern science differ markedly, though their meanings are essentially the same. The religious vocabulary seems dignified but archaic; our scientific vocabulary, persuasive but barbaric. "His id and Super-ego have not learned to cooperate," writes the modern

mental hygienist; "The flesh lusteth contrary to the spirit, and the spirit to the flesh," writes St. Paul. . . . "The capacity of the ego to ward off anxiety is enlarged if the ego has considerable affection for his fellows and a positive goal to help them." Correspondingly St. John writes, "Perfect love casteth out fear." It would be difficult, I suspect, to find any proposition in modern mental hygiene that has not been expressed with venerable symbols in some portion of the world's religious literature.

It turns out that in many respects psychological science and religion, for all their differences in vocabulary, have similar views regarding the origin, nature, and cure for mental distress. Where emphasis and technique differ the relationship between psychotherapy and religion can often be regarded as one of desirable supplementation. (pp. 109-10)

Here Allport suggests that psychology and religion are really expressing the same truths. They are simply using a different set of symbols to express them. Although this conciliatory viewpoint is a marked improvement in comparison to the Against model, it really does away with the possibility of genuine integration. Since psychology and religion are already saying the same thing, the need is for us to *translate*, not integrate. The unstated assumption seems to be that there is nothing really unique or new to come from the interaction of psychology and religion—only greater clarification and improved communication.

THE PARALLELS MODEL (SACRED VERSION) The Christian version of the Parallels model emphasizes the importance of both Scripture and psychology. But like its secular counterpart, it assumes either explicitly or implicitly that the two do not deeply interact. Paul Clement's (Note 2) description of the relation of psychology and theology is representative of the isolationist perspective. He writes:

Students of inferential statistics learn a concept which is very useful in solving a fundamental problem in the integration of psychology and theology. It is the concept of orthogonal relationships. Two factors are orthogonally related, if they are independent or uncorrelated. For example, within the psychological dimension intelligence and extraversion are orthogonal. Knowing how bright or dull a person is in no way suggests how outgoing or withdrawn he may be. There are many orthogonal factors within psychology. Knowing where a person scores along each psychological factor provides information about the individual which could not be obtained from any other orthogonally related factor. Each orthogonal factor expands our knowledge of the person; the more orthogonal factors, the better.

Not only are there many orthogonal factors within psychology, there are many orthogonal relationships between psychology and other disciplines. Each philosophical perspective is represented by one or more disciplines. When two or more disciplines come out of the same philosophical perspective, they may be nonorthogonal, i.e., correlated or interdependent. When two disciplines come out of two different philosophical perspectives, they are necessarily orthogonal. Such is the case with psychology and theology.

As with all orthogonally related disciplines, psychology and theology are complementary. Both add to a more complete picture of man's experience. Logically they cannot contradict each other, since contradictions can only take place within a perspective. Clashes between perspectives can only produce pseudo-contradictions.

Clement stresses the validity of the scientific study of both psychology and theology. By carefully relegating each discipline to the confines of its own methodology, language, and perspectives, the problem of potential conflicts between psychology and theology is easily resolved. There can be no conflicts because psychology and theology are independent and uncorrelated. But this solution, so deceptively simple, also rules out the possibility of integration. Such isolation destroys integration; for if psychology and theology are orthogonally related, there can be no meaningful interaction.

An essentially correlational viewpoint can be seen in *What Then Is Man?* (1958). The contributors to this volume outline a solid theological view of salvation and other basic Christian doctrines and then proceed to discuss three psychological views of conversion and the implications for the orthodox biblical view. The theology never wavers, but it is as if the theology is on one side of a chasm and the psychology on the other. There is an attempt to build a bridge, but at the same time there is a lack of certainty about where to anchor the bridge on the psychological side.

Many Christian therapists either wittingly or unwittingly adopt this approach. Trained in the better secular institutions of the day, they generally practice the type of psychology they have learned during graduate study. As Christians they desire to relate their faith to their academic and professional endeavors, but perhaps because of a lack of theological sophistication they fail to move beyond a correlational approach. Clyde Narramore's *Psychology of Counseling* (1960) is an early evangelical example of this approach. The first portion of the book is essentially a discussion of Rogerian principles of counseling. For example, he writes:

> A counselor may help a counselee discover and follow his own unique pattern by observing the following:
> - Provide a place and atmosphere conducive to uninterrupted discussion.
> - Encourage the counselee to talk and express himself freely.
> - Reflect and restate what the counselee says, thereby encouraging him to clarify his own thoughts and to say more.
> - Do not register surprise at any information which the counselee reveals.
> - Refrain from censoring or judging what the counselee says.
> - Encourage the counselee to suggest and discuss his own possible solutions.
> - Maintain a confidential attitude toward all discussion. (p. 57)

Along with this summary of some of the fundamentals of nondirective counseling there is a discussion of specific problems a pastoral counselor is likely to encounter and a listing of relevant Scripture references. There is, then, a general discussion of counseling principles and a discussion of the use of Scripture, but there is no real integration at a conceptual level.

Other authors have seen correlations between psychoanalysis and Christian theology. Barkman (1965), for example, writes:

> In contrasting the successful, integrated person with the double-minded unsuccessful and unhappy person, James says that the latter goes to the mirror of God's Word, "glances at himself and goes away, and at once forgets what he looked like" (1:24 NEB). Having seen himself in the light of his standard of values, he promptly repressed what he saw. To be sure, James does not use the word "repress," but he uses the "forgot" in such a way that it

fits rather easily into the psychologist's concept of brushing knowledge aside because it is unpleasant. . . . Psychoanalytic theory holds that it may have been conscious at one time, or it need never have been conscious at all. . . . What James says clearly is that there exists a state of affairs in some of his readers, in which these Christian people are not seeing themselves for what they really are. Somehow, what they read and understand about themselves doesn't sink in, but is passed off without integration into the personality. . . . In a sense James meets his readers at the same point where the psychotherapist meets his patient. (pp. 62-64)

And Sall (1975) writes:

Let us evaluate and compare this psychoanalytic material with Scripture. The Bible teaches that "the heart is deceitful above all things, and desperately corrupt" (Jeremiah 17:9). The "heart" in this context corresponds to what the Bible describes as the "old self" (Romans 6:6) or what the theologian calls the "old nature," which men inherited from Adam and which is very similar to what the psychologist terms the "uncontrollable id impulses." . . . Paul describes the conflict arising from these impulses gone awry: "I do not know what I am doing. For what I want to do I do not do, but what I hate I do. . . . I know that nothing good lives in me, but I cannot carry it out. . . . What a wretched man I am! Who will rescue me from this body of death?" (Romans 7:15, 18, 24). Paul conceded that his ego at times was overwhelmed by these id impulses, but the saving grace of God through Christ helped him to overcome sin.

Conversion changes man's desires, but it doesn't rid him of temptation. The tempted ego receives a boost from God, who functions like a great Superego, so the person will not yield to temptation. (pp. 22-23)

In these passages we see James's concept of forgetting equated with repression, the heart equated with the id, Paul's concept of "I" with the ego, and God likened to a great Superego.

But it is not only Rogerians and psychoanalysts who have attempted to find parallels between a current psychological system and Scripture. Drakeford (1967) does the same thing for Glasser's reality therapy and Mowrer's integrity therapy. While going beyond these authors in some regards, his basic approach is to find parallels between their teachings and those of Christianity.

Having looked at some representative Parallels viewpoints, we are now in a position to see more clearly the essential ingredients of this approach. At its foundation the Parallels model is rooted in the belief that Christianity and psychology are not intrinsically related. Each exists in its own sphere. Psychology is scientific while Christianity is personal (or social). Both Christianity and psychology can be embraced without fear of conflict since they operate in different spheres. Where we do find areas of relationship and overlap, we view these more as interesting parallels than as indicators of a deeper (or broader) unifying set of truths that could conceivably embrace both disciplines.

SUMMARY AND EVALUATION   Table 6 summarizes the essential premises of the isolation version of the Parallels model.

TABLE 6—THE PARALLELS MODEL (ISOLATION)

SECULAR	SACRED
• Religion and psychology are not related. Each exists in its own sphere.	• Religion and psychology are not related. Each exists in its own sphere.
• Psychology is scientific and objective while religion is personal and social.	• Psychology is scientific and objective while religion is personal and social.
• Psychology's goal is personal wholeness, but this does not include the redemptive aspects of Scripture.	• Redemptive as well as the creative-providential aspects of Christianity are stressed.
• Religion can be embraced since it belongs to a different sphere.	• Psychology can be embraced since it belongs to a different sphere.
• Religious problems should be referred to religious practitioners.	• Psychological problems should be referred to psychological practitioners.

We can summarize the sacred version of the correlation model as follows:

- Psychology and Christianity are two separate spheres of knowledge.
- The two spheres have their own sources of truth (scientific method and revelation), their own methods of investigation (experimentation and exegesis), and their own data (psychological principles and facts, and biblical principles and facts).
- Integration consists of finding the concepts that are parallel (equivalent) in the other discipline (sphere).
- The parallels between the two disciplines (spheres) regarding the nature of the human being, pathology, or therapies, that are developed must never lose or violate the autonomous character of either discipline (sphere).
- There is a tendency for the correlation model to break down in practice so that spiritual problems are handled by the pastor and psychological problems are handled by the psychologist or psychiatrist. That is, the correlation model has an internal tension that tends to break down into an isolation model or occasionally move in the opposite direction toward a genuine integration model.

The correlation version has no clear secular counterpart because non-Christian theorists do not accept the Bible as an authoritative source of truth and are generally not interested in the redemptive aspects of Scripture that set psychology and theology off as two separate spheres of knowledge and/or experience. Some secular proponents of the Of model approach a correlationist position, but their reinterpretation of Scripture to fit into their psychological theorizing destroys the unity and integrity of theology as a separate sphere of knowledge and consequently places them in an Of rather than a correlation model.

The Parallels model has several basic strengths. It is an obvious improvement over the Against model in that it drops the antagonistic rhetoric and oppositional stance of that model. In emphasizing the distinctiveness of psychology and theology as separate disciplines, the isolationist version of the Parallels model also preserves the integrity of both disciplines and avoids superficial attempts at integration. The correlation version of the Parallels model has the added advantage of moving in the direction of true integration. It is frequently a good starting point. In fact, in some instances a parallel study may be the only pragmatic way to begin the process of integration. Before unifying concepts can be found, there has to be an initial lining up of overlapping issues and concerns. Once this has been done, we can move to a deeper level of integration.[1]

The Parallels model does, however, have serious limitations. It is based on the assumption that we are dealing with two separate entities that can at best be lined up to find common meaning, and this assumption precludes true and comprehensive integration. This is its most basic fault. It cannot produce the broader unifying principles that are necessary for true integration because of its artificial separation of sources of truth.

There is another weakness in the correlation version of the Parallels model. In attempting to find common ground between psychology and theology, it lends itself to the practice of forcing the data of one discipline arbitrarily upon that of another. For our present purposes we are not concerned with the accuracy of the parallels cited above. It may well be that the biblical understanding of conscience comes close to Freud's concept of the superego. And it may well be that we need to provide an accepting and nonjudgmental atmosphere in therapy. Our point is not that these are inaccurate but rather that they lack the comprehensiveness that is embodied in a unifying set of principles or concepts and that they

[1]Portions of chapter 3 of this volume are written from an essentially Parallels position. Although we assume there are broad unifying principles in each area of overlap between psychology and theology, we have not attempted to pursue all of them. Instead, the potential areas of integration are simply listed as parallels or possibilities for integration. While this method demonstrates the potential scope of integration, it is only a starting point. If true integration is to be done, this lining up of overlapping concerns must be followed by a careful study of these relationships and a search for unifying principles.

may lead to an inaccurate psychologizing of Scripture or a superficial Christianizing of psychology. It is this weakness in the Parallels model that Adams (1970) rejects in his attempt to build a biblical view of counseling. If we are not careful, our understanding of Christian psychology is simply a Christianized version of one or another secular psychological theory.

THE
INTEGRATES MODEL

Using the Against, Of, and **7** Parallels models as a backdrop, we are now prepared to look at the potential for a truly comprehensive integra- tion of psychology and theology. We call this the Integrates model.

The sacred version of the Integrates model is rooted in the assumption that God is the author of all truth. Reason, revelation, and the scientific method all are seen as playing a valid role in the search for truth. Since the human being is created in the image of God and since God has revealed Himself in a special way through Scripture and in a general way through creation, we expect to find congruence between Scripture and the findings of psychology.

Since humanity has fallen into sin and God's image in us has been marred, the integrationist does not assume that all the truth claims made by psychologists are valid. But neither does this person presume to have an infallible interpretation of Scripture. When God created humanity, He created the possibility for psychology. The Integrates approach emphasizes both psychology and the Scriptures because they are allies. Psychology here is the psychology that existed before the word was coined, while *Psychology* in the other three models refers to a theory or a system.

Believing in the unity of truth, proponents of the Integrates model do not look at psychological and theological understandings as distinct fields of study that are essentially unrelatable. Instead, they assume that since God is the Author of all truth, and since He is the Creator of the entire world, there is ultimately only one set of explanatory hypotheses. While the methods and data of psychology are frequently distinct (and the distinctions need to be maintained), followers of the Integrates model are looking for unifying concepts that will broaden the understanding that would come from either psychology or theology in isolation. In other words, they search for integrative principles without violating the methodology or level of analysis of either.

THE INTEGRATES MODEL (SECULAR VERSION) Given this definition of the Integrates model, it can be seen that no secular approach to the interface of theology and psychology can be fully integrative. Since secular authors do not hold to the existence of a personal God who has revealed Himself through nature and His Word, they cannot be truly committed to the unity of the truths of science and those of biblical revelation. Secular theorists may follow an Of model or even a correlational version of the Parallels model, but they cannot follow a fully integrated model as we have defined it here. To do that requires a full commitment to both the learned facts of psychology and the revealed truths of Scripture.

It is this epistemological assumption along with a commitment to the unity of truth under the Creator that is the foundation for a comprehensive integration. And it is this commitment that proponents of the Against, Of, and Parallels models lack to one degree or another. This is not to minimize the contributions of secular theorists. It is simply to say that for those committed to an orthodox view of Scripture, no fully integrative approach to truth can be undertaken without a commitment to the God of scriptural revelation. The apostle Paul put it this way:

The man without the Spirit does not accept the things that come from the Spirit of God, for they are foolishness to him, and he cannot understand them, because they are spiritually discerned. The spiritual man makes judgments about all things, but he himself is not subject to any man's judgment: "For who has known the mind of the Lord that he may instruct him?" (1 Cor. 2:14-16)

Secular theorists such as Mowrer, Fromm, Thorne, and Allport may see religion as an integrative force in personal living. They may stress religion's contributions to personal adjustment and maturity. They may draw upon religion's emphasis on the spirit and the inner life of the human being. They may support a rapprochement of psychology and religion. And they may see great insights for personal living in the Scriptures. But in spite of their contribution to our understanding of the relationships between psychology and religion, they are limited because they lack insight into and commitment to the Bible as God's authoritative revelation.

THE INTEGRATES MODEL (SACRED VERSION) Although the last decade has seen the development of a vast popular literature on psychology and the Scriptures, there is still a significant lack of truly integrative writings on psychology and theology. In fact, it is sometimes difficult to distinguish between the correlation version of the Parallels model and genuine integration in this popular literature because the goal of these writings is to promote practical Christian living rather than conceptual understanding. Consequently we have few writings that have tried to grapple in a deep or comprehensive way with the integration of psychology and theology.[1] In the remainder of this chapter we will lay out the assumptions that underlie an integrative approach to the study of psychology and theology and illustrate the outworking of these assumptions in the writings of several authors who seem to us to be following a fruitful approach to integration.

[1] Much of the technical work exploring the nature and the content of the integration of psychology and the Scripture appears in two periodicals, *The Journal of the American Scientific Affiliation* and the *Journal of Psychology and Theology.* Many members of the Christian Association for Psychological Studies are also actively pursuing an integrative approach.

The Unity of Truth

William Hulme is one of the best representatives of the Integrates model. In his discussion of the dangers of scientism (1956), we have a good illustration of the outworking of one of the basic propositions of the Integrates model—the unity of truth.

> What was once a danger of antiscience within the church has become the danger of scientism. This is particularly true regarding the doctrine of man. Too often it seems that the thirst for the approval of the intelligentsia has led churchmen to the unscientific assumption that the present stage of science is supreme, even against their own Bible evidence. A more objective approach would weigh each on its own merits, especially since the theories of evolution within the natural sciences have themselves been undergoing continuous realignment to the discoveries of new and sometimes disturbing evidence. (p. 98)

Hulme shows that he is not content with the psychologizing of Scripture found in the Of or Parallels (correlational) models. He believes the church is in danger of elevating the theories of science to a place of authority above Scripture, which would destroy Christianity's unique contribution to our understanding of the human being. At the same time he is not suggesting that we minimize or neglect the findings of science. He suggests that we should weigh the contributions of both science and the Bible.

Crabb (1975) offers a similar suggestion:

> Now if Christians are to realize the vision of displacing secular counseling with a biblical approach . . . we must neither minimize these doctrinal essentials nor stop with them. Evangelicals often do one or the other. It simply is not enough to inform a depressed person that he is sinful and that he must confess his sin to Christ and stop living sinfully. Such an approach presents Christianity as oppressive rather than liberating. . . .
>
> We must develop a solidly biblical approach to counseling, one which draws from secular psychology without betraying its Scriptural premise. (pp. 17-18)

Running throughout this statement is a commitment to the unity of truth. Crabb assumes that the truths of secular psychology will not be in conflict with the Scripture. He assumes that Scripture has a great deal to say about counseling. And he assumes that a study of both psychology and the Scriptures will give us a more complete understanding of the human personality than either in isolation.

Paul Tournier's *Guilt and Grace* (1962) is another integrative approach that shows a natural commitment to the unity of truth. He writes:

> Thus the true guilt of men comes from the things with which they are reproached by God in their innermost hearts. Only they can discover what these things are. And they are usually very different from the things with which they are reproached by men. The reference to God brought to us by the Bible illuminates our problem in a remarkable way, from now on, "false guilt" is that which comes as a result of the judgments and suggestions of men. "True guilt" is that which results from divine judgment. (p. 67)

Tournier gives us a way of reconciling the psychologist's understanding of the nature of neurotic guilt and its origins in relationships with others with the scriptural emphasis on human response to divine conviction. This distinction is now so widely accepted that we can easily forget how new it was in many circles when Tournier first started addressing the issue twenty-five years ago.

The Nature of the Human Being

One of the fundamental assumptions of those following an integrative model has to do with the nature of the human being. Personhood, for the integrationist, is rooted in the fact that the human being is created in the image of God. All thinking about the human being is colored by the view we take of human origin and destiny. And it is here that the integrationist finds a major starting place in building a comprehensive view of personhood. The human being is created in the image of God but has also fallen into sin. These twin assumptions influence all other thinking the integrationist does about human personality. They set the stage for the rest of the integrationist's understandings and serve as basic underlying principles.

An excerpt from Hulme's *Counseling and Theology* (1967)

demonstrates the significance integrationists place on the understanding of human nature.

> The Christian concept of man is more or less fundamental to this theological correlation, as it deals with the nature and interpretation of the conflict in human personality that gives rise to the destructive emotions. This conflict is identified by the doctrine as the conflict between the way a man is and the way he was meant to be—between the image of God in which God created him and the corruption of that image in sin. Regardless of what particular confession we consult the doctrine of man has these two parts: man as God created him and man as he has become; the image of God, and the corruption of this image. (p. 95)

These dual facts affect almost every area of the relationship of psychology and theology.

Since the image of God carries with it the assumption that humans are spiritual beings, a commitment to the concept of the human being as a fallen image-bearer influences our view of the nature of truth about and the appropriate methods for studying humanity. It means that naturalistic methods of study can never fully explain the nature of human personhood since humans are spiritual beings. The assumption that we are image-bearers also influences our thinking about determinism and free will. Since the Scriptures state that God is a free moral agent and that we are in His image, this means that we must also, in some very basic respect, be free moral agents. And viewing the human being as an image-bearer also speaks to self-acceptance and to other's right to self-respect.

The assumption that humanity is fallen leads to a cautious attitude about all methodologies and "facts" since we realize that human reason is less than perfect. It influences our view of psychopathology since it carries with it a concept of both personal and corporate sin and consequently of both personal and corporate responsibility. It leads to certain assumptions about the resolution of guilt feelings. And it limits our acceptance of the optimistic predictions of some humanistic thinkers. In every area of psychological theory, the biblical view of the human being has important implications.

The Origin of Psychopathology

A discussion of the essentials of human nature leads us logically to the next major assumption of proponents of an Integrates model. This is the assumption that in the ultimate sense all psychopathology is traceable to sin. By this we do not mean that all problems are caused by conscious, willful, or personal sins but that all problems ultimately are traceable to the split in human nature that came with the first sin. Hulme (1967), for example, writes:

> Man's decision to participate in the temptation to rebel introduced evil into his nature. The radical contrast between this new experience and the original righteousness in which he was created, produced a violent reaction, a clash-in-the-gears, as it were. This is evidenced by the release of the destructive emotions which not only perpetuate but increase this division. Becoming a part of his personality this division influences every activity of his personality—the ambiguity between sin and righteousness is characteristic of his being. Consequently the doctrine of man is not concerned with sins but sin. Individual sins are merely the peripheral manifestation of this inner corruption of the imago Dei. (p. 105)

In Hulme's view, Scripture brings a unifying understanding to our view of personal maladjustments. Psychological maladjustment is not simply the result of childhood conditioning. It is not simply the result of parental mistreatment. And it is not simply the result of wrong choices or wrong actions. While all of these enter in, in the most basic sense, psychological disturbances originate in a split within the personality—a split that results in alienation from God, ourselves, and others. Thus the psychological understanding of the human being's inner conflict is clarified, elaborated, and brought into perspective when it is traced ultimately to the conflict between the attempt to be what the creature was intended to be (an image-bearer) and the desire to fulfill a corrupted understanding of this image.

The Balanced Use of Scripture

Consistent with their emphasis on the biblical view of the nature of the human being, those following an Integrates approach also maintain a balanced view of Scripture. In contrast to the Of model's selective use of the creative and providential aspects of Scripture, proponents of an integrative approach accept the totality of biblical revelation and its relevance to constructive living. Consequently the redemptive and supernatural aspects of Scripture are given equal emphasis with the creative and providential aspects. Proponents of an integrative approach do not shy away from the Scripture's emphasis on human alienation from God and the need of salvation. Neither do they see prayer as simply a spiritualized form of emotional catharsis. Wagner (1974), for example, writes:

> When we experience spiritual conversion, we enter into a personal relationship with God which corrects the problem of omnipotence within our psyche. We stop belonging to ourselves and we start belonging to God. We have yielded the essential right to our own omnipotence, and we have accepted God as our omnipotent one. Because of this commitment, we can experience a freedom from guilt (Romans 8:1) by His forgiveness. (pp. 81-82)

Wagner acknowledges the reality of humanity's need of redemption and demonstrates one of the psychological benefits of this experience. Spiritual conversion is seen not as a simple religious metaphor for change but as an actual change in one's inner being based on the redemptive work of Christ and the work of the Holy Spirit.

Respect for the Uniqueness of Other Disciplines

One reason some psychologists and theologians have shied away from an integrative study is the concern that their particular discipline might be weakened, watered down, or forced into a mold. Theologians, for example, are rightly skeptical of an Of or Parallels approach to integration that reinterprets Scripture or forces psychological concepts on the Bible in an arbitrary manner. Similarly, psychologists reject attempts at integration that suggest that psychology as a discipline really has nothing unique to offer—it is simply an intellectual way of stating what the Bible has told us all along.

Proponents of an Integrates model do not attempt to press data, methods, or theory into areas where they do not fit. They have a keen sensitivity to this problem and take care to distinguish between different levels of analysis and to preserve the unique methodology and content of each discipline. Carlson (Note 1) put it this way:

> I see us Christian professionals caught between those who would transform psychology into theology and those who would transform theology into psychology. To me the process and problem of integration is quite different. I conceive of integration to be the conscious bringing together of the component aspects of psychology and theology with our violating their individual autonomy or identity and without ignoring conflict, paradox, and mystery. In this view, integration is more than baptizing psychology without scriptural texts or lining up psychology and theology to see their points of correlation and convergence.

And Hulme (1967) writes:

> While it may seem that theology traces the source of man's predicament to his sin and clinical psychology speaks only of guilt, the difference is primarily one of approach. In the doctrine of man guilt is revealed as the first of many consequences that show why rebellion (sin) is wrong. In the designation sin, the theology of the church gives expression to the dualistic conception of life that characterizes the biblical record. Psychology, dealing primarily with the reactions of personality, is concerned with the guilt reaction to what the individual feels is sin rather than any metaphysical analysis of good and evil. Since guilt may be both genuine and neurotic it is obvious that the nature of sin is outside the realm of psychology. (p. 155)

Hulme shows that we need to maintain a clear understanding of our levels of analysis and points out that our theological understanding of sin invokes a metaphysical analysis while the psychologist's concern is more of a focus on the experience of guilt rather than the metaphysics of sin. This type of differentiation helps preserve the autonomy of both psychology and theology as legitimate fields of study but also makes possible an integration that involves both the broader theological or metaphysical understanding and the psychological. He suggests that we should weigh the contributions of both science and the Bible.

Christianity and Mental Health

Proponents of an Integrates model operate on the assumption that truly biblical religion is in no way detrimental to good mental hygiene. In fact, they assume that living that is in accordance with divine revelation will be a significant factor in promoting personal growth and wholeness.

Maurice Wagner (1975) illustrates this truth in *The Sensation of Being Somebody*. While Wagner's perspective is strongly influenced by psychoanalytic thinking, it seems obvious that he has not attempted to press a psychoanalytic view of personality onto the data of Scripture. Instead, he has allowed Scripture to serve as an integrating frame of reference. The result is a most stimulating viewpoint that reflects some excellent integrative thinking. Speaking of the role of faith in handling feelings of hostility he writes:

> Faith in Christ provides an answer to the problem of hostility as well as of guilt. When we accept His sovereignty, we accept His ownership of all things, including ourselves. He is sovereign over our situation as well as over our minds. We trust God never to forsake us. That does not mean that God will keep us from pain or misery or death. It means that we have a hope in Him that extends beyond this life to eternity. The injustices we find here will be equalized at the Day of Judgment.
>
> Our hostility functions on the basis of our sense of prerogative to do whatever we want as though we owned all things. Our faith in God surrenders that sense of prerogative to Him so that we are willing to accept the vicissitudes of life without resentment over the unpleasant. Ordinarily, we want everything to be pleasant and we tend to resent anything that we don't like. Our faith in God and identification with the sufferings of Christ have taught us that life here cannot provide everything pleasant. Hardship can be beneficial, for in it we can grow more mature spiritually and emotionally. We know He suffered for us, and if He chooses to allow hardship, we can suffer for Him and do so as an expression of love. (pp. 86-87)

For Wagner the sovereignty of God is not a tidy intellectual concept; it is a scriptural truth that has many ramifications for our emotional functioning. Similarly, the resolution of negative feelings of anger is not relegated to a secular therapeutic process. Our understanding of the significance of the sovereignty of God is part of the process of resolving destructive emotions.

From a somewhat different perspective van Kaam (1968) also stresses the role of religion as an integrative and healing force in life. He writes:

> Religious personality refers to a personality in which the religious mode of existence is the most central mode of being and which integrates and permeates all other ways of being in the world. The religious personality therefore incorporates all the characteristics of what we may call authentic personality. The only difference is that the religious concern is ultimate in the religious personality—just as some other concern may be central to another type of personality. (p. 58)

Here we have a very natural statement about the central integrating role of religious experience in the believer's life. Integration is not simply an intellectual exercise. It is a personal process that orients one's entire life.

Christianity and Psychotherapy

When we come to the topic of counseling and therapy we find a wide range of opinions among therapists equally committed to scriptural revelation. Even among therapists who follow an integrative model we find those leaning toward client-centered (Hulme, 1967), rational-emotive (Crabb, 1977), analytic (Wagner, 1975), and existential (van Kaam, 1968) styles of counseling.

At first glance this seems surprising. Shouldn't Christian therapists who are committed to the authority of Scripture be able to agree on one general model of counseling? Isn't the Bible sufficiently precise to show us *the* biblical approach to counseling?

As desirable as this may be, for a variety of reasons we doubt that this will every happen. To begin with, the nature of people's adjustment problems dictates the counseling style that will be most helpful. Short-term, directive counseling is ready-made for a variety of situational problems and certain personalities. Long-term therapy may be very helpful for others. Behavioral methods are clearly successful in relieving a variety of symptoms. And many people respond well to nondirective counseling. The variety of effective therapeutic styles suggests that no one counseling methodology will serve all purposes.

Jesus demonstrated a very flexible approach to people's problems. The contrast between His treatment of the woman taken in adultery (John 8:3-11) and the moneychangers in the temple (Mark 11:15-19) is a good example. He apparently did not find that one style of relating fit every situation. Carlson (Note 1) suggests the following division between prophetic and priestly approaches to counseling.

Prophetic	Priestly
Convicting	Comforting
Confronting	Confessional
Preaching	Interviewing
Lecturing	Listening
Thinking for	Thinking with
Talking to	Talking with
Proclaiming truth	Affirming truth
Disturbing the comfortable	Comforting the disturbed

While some might see these roles as dichotomous or even contradictory, they are in fact reflecting the fact that different people have different needs and that these needs call for different styles of relating. To the degree this is true, we should expect a great deal of diversity within and between Christian counselors.

But if we look beyond these differences in styles of relating, we should find a great deal of congruence regarding underlying assumptions and basic issues in counseling. Christian therapists from a variety of orientations would agree, for example, that personal maladjustments are most effectively resolved when viewed holistically. They would agree that the influence of both personal and corporate sin in a counselee's life should be explored. They would agree that the counselor functions as an agent of reconciliation, and they would agree that guilt feelings are in some way related to sin.

What we are suggesting is this: We should expect Christian counselors and therapists to differ in their specific counseling styles and in certain areas of understanding. They will vary, for example, in the direct use (quoting or reading) of Scripture in counseling.

Some will readily share specific biblical texts with counselees. Others may never do this. The latter will use Scripture in formulating an understanding of their counselee's problems and appropriate counseling approaches, but because they are committed to a less directive counseling style, they focus more on the counselee's difficulty in appropriating truths they already know intellectually than on imparting new information. In either case, integrative therapists' understanding of their counselees, their conceptual formulation of the problems, and their commitment to their counselees' growth is done within a scriptural context.

Unfortunately, many people equate Christian counseling only with the direct use of Scripture. This minimizes the importance of a broad biblical understanding of the human being, of the importance of the therapeutic relationship in producing growth, and of many other key ingredients of psychotherapy. Truly integrative therapists begin with this broad conceptual understanding and work toward specific counseling techniques.

As we approach specific techniques, we find increasing differences of opinion both because of different personality styles and because of the Scriptures' relatively minimal discussion of counseling techniques. The Scriptures are very specific on issues like the nature of the human being, sin, guilt, anxiety, and a variety of other problems, attitudes, and actions. Because of this we can expect a great deal of agreement on fundamental issues and on the general parameters of Christian counseling. We must take care, however, not to confuse the outward forms or styles of counseling with their inner substance.

Proponents of an Integrates model will not neglect the outer form and style, but they will nevertheless focus on more central issues such as the role of sin in psychopathology, the place of personal and societal responsibility, the role of the Holy Spirit in sanctification, and the importance of deep caring relationships in promoting personal growth. Based upon our understanding of basic issues such as these, we will select the counseling methodology that seems best suited to our own personalities and that will allow us to help others move toward the biblical goal of maturity.

THE PROCESS OF INTEGRATION

8

By now it should be apparent that from our perspective integration is more than simply a matter of relating separate subject areas. Integration can be thought of in a threefold manner. It is, of course, the relating of Christian and secular concepts. But it is more than that. It is also a way of thinking and a way of functioning.

So far we have focused largely on integration as the relating of secular and Christian concepts. But underneath our discussion is the assumption that integration is also a way of living and a way of thinking. In fact, it seems to us that very little conceptual integration is possible without a degree of personal integration. That is, unless we as persons are open to the impact of a relationship with God in our lives and unless we are open to seeing our own maladaptive ways of coping, we will find it necessary to shut ourselves off from certain sources of truth and block any real progress in integration. In fact, this is perhaps the biggest single barrier to integration. It is far too easy to ensconce ourselves securely behind the walls of our theological or psychological professionalism in order to avoid facing the truth about ourselves and consequently being open to new perspectives.

We all find security in our traditional ways of viewing things and tend to be threatened by new or different ideas and perceptions. The pastor who has years of training and experience in viewing maladjustment as sin may be threatened by the psychologist's view that this is really a psychological disturbance. And the psychologist has no less difficulty with the pastor's view than what the psychologist calls pathology is really sin. It is no easy task to move beyond our initial anxiety, defensiveness, and even resentment at representatives of other disciplines and begin to develop a truly integrative way of looking at things.

While there is no simple way to overcome these anxieties, it seems to us that there are a few attitudes and attributes that are essential in allowing us the freedom to pursue a truly integrative approach. Humility and an awareness of finite limitations are certainly two of the most basic. Van Kaam (1968) writes:

> My humble suspicion of the taint of selfish impulse keeps alive in me the need for redemption. I shall humbly accept that my motives are not fully transparent to me because I am not a pure spirit, but a fallen human being in need of purification. I shall be satisfied with a peaceful pondering of my intentions within the limits of reason and possibility. The rest I leave to God in surrender. (p. 141)

Van Kaam is sensitive to his own fallibility and the limitation of human understanding. While he is one of the most active proponents of an integration of psychology and theology, he also realizes that the answer might not be immediately forthcoming. This attitude of humility allows us to be open to the view of others and to new ways of looking at human behavior. Without this no significant progress will be made at integration.

Closely related to humility is the ability to tolerate ambiguity. In a new and essentially pioneering venture it is essential to keep an open mind. We must be able to see alternative perspectives, look for new relationships, and, above all, not be too quick to throw aside apparently conflicting information. It is out of seeming contradictions and unresolvable dilemmas that new insights frequently emerge. If we attempt to close the book on integration, we shut off this process of personal creativity. Van Kaam (1968) speaks of this while discussing the actualization of various dimensions of the personality.

> The encounter between the personality and the world actualizes many modes of existence. As the person develops, some modes of existence may seem incompatible with one another. He accepts this seeming incompatibility temporarily, however, until he is able to reconcile the different modes of existence from a higher viewpoint. The highest mode of existence for the religious person is commitment to the divine. (p. 99)

Integrationists such as van Kaam are able to tolerate ambiguity while still looking for unifying principles. They are able to hold seeming conflicts in abeyance or in tension until a broader perspective or a new way of looking at things brings resolution. This is a virtue that most Against theorists seem to lack. In being anxious to find the answers, they make closure too early and shut themselves off from insights available from differing perspectives.

A third personal characteristic that is basic to effective integration is a balanced expression of one's intellect and emotions. Our perceptions, thinking, construction of theories, interpretations of Scripture, and styles of counseling are all highly influenced by our intellectual and emotional style of living. Some of us favor a cognitive, intellectual style. We stress ideas, concepts, facts, and data. If we are theologians, we stress what the Word teaches. We emphasize right doctrine. And we don't give a large place to feeling and emotions. Some churches, in fact, are built almost exclusively around a ministry of teaching. Intimate fellowship, exalting and uplifting worship, and emotional expression have little if any place. In fact, they may even be discouraged. They are viewed as signs of weakness, immaturity, or lack of doctrinal grounding.

If we are psychologists, we express our cognitive style in other ways. We stress right actions and right thoughts. We become teachers who show others how to think. If they think properly, we reason, everything else will fall into place. Cognitive behavior modification and rational-emotive psychotherapy are two therapeutic approaches that lean in this direction.

Conversely, there are other pastors and psychologists who are strongly affectively oriented. Pastors with this style stress interpersonal involvement, worship, fellowship, and expression of emotions. And psychologists with this personality style focus almost exclusively on feelings. Thoughts are unimportant. They are defensive and inhibitory. We need to put them behind us and learn to feel—to get in touch with our true selves. Gestalt therapies and some group- and client-centered therapies lean heavily in this direction.

What is needed is a balanced perspective that is based on a healthy personal integration of the affective and cognitive sides of life. Far too often we assume that our interpretation of the Christian life is biblical without asking how our own personality style influenced and distorted our understanding. In fact, we all would probably be frightened if we knew how much of our psychological theorizing and our biblical interpretation was a reflection of our own personality style rather than either the data of psychology or the truths of biblical revelation. We need to realize that Christ was both a thinking and a feeling person and that we cannot have a truly balanced understanding of human nature unless we are open to both of these avenues of experience in ourselves and others. The more open we are to all aspects of experience, the more we will be able to gain a complete and accurate understanding of scriptural truth.

Our discussion of the role of humility, tolerance for ambiguity, and the balance of the affective and cognitive leads us to what is perhaps the major hurdle to deeply integrative thinking. This is our own personal anxiety and consequent defensiveness, which forces us to be less than fully open to the truth about ourselves and others. Our lack of humility, our inability to tolerate ambiguity, and our tendency to overemphasize either affect or cognition are all a result of our own inner anxieties and fears. We become rigid, closed, or intolerant because we fear the consequences of openness. We have learned that it is safer to restrict our awareness. To be open means to see our faults. It means acknowledging our failures. And it means being open to those around us.

All of these are potentially threatening; so we develop ways of defending against and warding off anxiety. "Theologians are too cognitive and intellectual," the psychologists say as they attempt to put theologians in a box and avoid their own anxiety about concepts of guilt, sin, and condemnation. "Psychologists are too experience oriented," retort the theologians as they try to dismiss theories that would bring too much intimacy or openness. And in both cases we are running from our own conflicts and short-circuiting any possibility of a true integration. We find it safer to restrict ourselves to our area of expertise and to our professional role. We are comfortable with our pulpit, couch, desk, or laboratory equipment, and we hesitate to venture out.

But we must venture out if we are going to build a meaningful integration. We need more empirical data to shed light on innumerable problems confronting the church. We need new scriptural insights and new theoretical concepts to understand better the nature of the human being and human functioning. And we need increasing application of our research, theory, and biblical interpretation. But if these are pursued in an isolated fashion, we will make very little progress. We must be willing to step out and ask new questions. We must be willing to reevaluate the answers that have been given to some old questions. And most of all, we must be willing to bring all conceivable sources of understanding to bear on our study of the human being and the human dilemma.

One last point seems especially important. As Christians our aim must not be simply to pursue isolated intellectual understanding. The clear message of Scripture is that God intervened in history to change lives. We need to see ourselves fulfilling a role in this divine plan in order to gain much-needed motivation and perspective. Integrative efforts come alive when we recognize their eternal aspect and see our work as part of humanity's God-ordained task of reconciling men to God, themselves, and others.

While scientism would dismiss such personal commitment as a violation of objectivity, it can be shown that total objectivity is a myth of science. It is impossible for our personal commitment to have no influence on the direction of our work. The decision to "be objective" and to exclude such concepts as God, faith, and repentance from the study of scientific psychology leads to a distorted perception of the human race. Under the guise of objective scientific methodology, we end up ignoring an essential side of human nature. At the same time we must not err in the opposite side—that of ignoring the data of psychology because of our scriptural focus.

As Christians we must reject both of these narrow views, and we can then affirm the broader biblical perspective that makes room for both scientific methodology and scriptural revelation. Rather than limiting or distorting our understanding, this commitment places our academic and professional careers in their broadest and truest perspective. An understanding of general revelation and the broad task of subduing the earth then becomes a divinely given task just as much as the proclamation of the gospel. It is at this point that integration enters in to look for a synthesis of roles, responsibilities, and ways of understanding God's creation.

REFERENCE LIST

Adams, J. *Competent to counsel.* Grand Rapids: Baker, 1970.

Adams, J. *The Christian counselor's manual.* Grand Rapids: Baker, 1973.

Allport, G. *The individual and his religion.* New York: Macmillan, 1950.

Barkman, P. *Man in conflict.* Grand Rapids: Zondervan, 1965.

Berkhouwer, G. C. *Man: The image of God.* Grand Rapids: Eerdmans, 1962.

Billheimer, P. *Don't waste your sorrows.* Fort Washington, Pa.: Christian Literature Crusade, 1977.

Boisen, A. *The exploration of the inner world.* Philadelphia: University of Pennsylvania Press, 1971. (Originally published, 1926.)

Buswell, J. O. *Systematic theology of the Christian religion.* Grand Rapids: Zondervan, 1962.

Carnell, E. J. *An introduction to Christian apologetics.* Grand Rapids: Eerdmans, 1948.

Carter, J. Maturity: Psychological and biblical. *Journal of Psychology and Theology,* 1974, 2, 89-96.

Chesen, E. S. *Religion may be hazardous to your health.* New York: Wyden, 1972.

Collins, G. The pulpit and the couch. *Christianity Today,* 1975, 19, 1087-1091.

Collins, G. *The rebuilding of psychology*. Wheaton: Tyndale, 1977.

Crabb, L. *Basic principles of biblical counseling*. Grand Rapids: Zondervan, 1975.

Crabb, L. *Effective biblical counseling*. Grand Rapids: Zondervan, 1977.

Dobson, J. *Dare to discipline*. Wheaton: Tyndale, 1970.

Drakeford, J. *Integrity therapy*. Nashville: Broadman, 1967.

Fenichel, O. *The psychoanalytic theory of neurosis*. New York: Norton, 1945.

Fosdick, H. *On being a real person*. New York: Harper and Row, 1943.

Freud, S. [*Totem and taboo*.] In A. Strackey (trans.), *The complete psychological works of Sigmund Freud*. Vol. 13, pp. 1-161. London: Hogarth, 1961. (Originally published, 1913.)

Freud, S. [*Future of an illusion*.] In A. Strackey (trans.), *The complete psychological works of Sigmund Freud*. Vol. 21, pp. 5-56. London: Hogarth, 1961. (Originally published, 1927.)

Fromm. E. *Psychoanalysis and religion*. New Haven, Conn.: Yale University Press, 1950.

Gaebelein, F. *The pattern of God's truth*. Chicago: Moody, 1968.

Gangel, K. Toward a biblical theology of marriage and family. *Journal of Psychology and Theology*, 1977, *5* (1-4).

Glasser, W. *Reality therapy*. New York: Harper and Row, 1965.

Gothard, B. *Institute in basic youth conflicts: Research in principles of life*. La Grange, Ill.: Basic Youth Conflicts, n.d.

Greenson, R. R. *The technique and practice of psychoanalysis*. New York: International Universities Press, 1967.

Hendricks, H. *Heaven help the home*. Wheaton: Victor, 1973.

Hession, R. *The calvary road*. Fort Washington, Pa.: Christian Literature Crusade, 1950.

Hiltner, S. *Theological dynamics*. Nashville: Abingdon, 1972.

Hodge, C. *Systematic theology*. Grand Rapids: Eerdmans, 1960. (Originally published, 1872.)

Holmes, A. *All truth is God's truth*. Grand Rapids: Eerdmans, 1977.

Horney, K. *Neurosis and human growth*. New York: Norton, 1950.

Hulme, W. *Counseling and theology*. Philadelphia: Fortress, 1956.

Hyder, Q. *The Christian's handbook of psychiatry*. Old Tappan, N.J.: Revell, 1971.

James, M., and Savary, L. *The Power at the bottom of the well: T.A. and religious experience*. New York: Harper and Row, 1974.

James, W. *The varieties of religious experience*. London: Longman's, 1952. (Originally published, 1901.)

Jeeves, M. *Psychology and Christianity: The view both ways*. Downers Grove, Ill.: InterVarsity, 1976.

Kaam, A. van. *Religion and personality*. New York: Doubleday, Image Books, 1968.

Kohlberg, L. The development of moral character and moral ideology. In Martin L. Hoffmann and Lois W. Hoffmann (Eds.), *Review of child development research* (Vol. 1). New York: Russell Sage Foundation, 1964.

Kraft, C. Can anthropological insight assist evangelical theology? *Christian Scholar's Review*, 1977, *7*, 165-202.

LaHaye, T. *Transformed temperaments*. Wheaton: Tyndale, 1971.

Linn, L., & Schwarz, L. *Psychiatry and religious experience*. New York: Random House, 1958.

Maslow, A. *Motivation and personality* (2nd ed.). New York: Harper and Row, 1970.

Meehl, P. (Ed.). *What, then, is man?* A symposium of theology, psychology, and psychiatry. St. Louis: Concordia, 1958.

Menninger, K. *Whatever became of sin?* New York: Hawthorn, 1975.

Miller, K. *The taste of new wine*. Waco: Word, 1965.

Mowrer, O. H. *The crisis in psychiatry and religion*. Princeton, N.J.: Van Nostrand, 1961.

Narramore, B. Parent leadership styles and biblical anthropology. *Bibliotheca Sacra*, 1978, *135*(540), 345-357.

Narramore, C. *The psychology of counseling*. Grand Rapids: Zondervan, 1960.

Ortlund, R. *Lord, make my life a miracle*. Glendale: Regal, 1974.

Petersen, B., and Broad, S. Unmasking: an interview with Waldon Howard. *Eternity*, August, 1977, *28*, 10-15.

Piaget, J. *The moral development of the child*. New York: Free, 1948.

Ramm, B. *The Christian view of science and Scripture*. Grand Rapids: Eerdmans, 1954.

Rogers, C. *Client-centered therapy*. Boston: Houghton-Mifflin, 1951.

Rychlak, J. F. *Introduction to personality and psychotherapy*. Boston: Houghton-Mifflin, 1972.

Sall, M. *Faith, psychology, and Christian maturity.* Grand Rapids: Zondervan, 1975.

Sanford, J. *Dreams: God's forgotten language.* Philadelphia: Lippincott, 1968.

Sauer, E. *The king of the earth.* London: Paternoster, 1962.

Schaeffer, F. *True spirituality.* Wheaton: Tyndale, 1971.

Skinner, B. F. *Beyond freedom and dignity.* New York: Knopf, 1971.

Small, D. *Christian: Celebrate your sexuality.* Old Tappan, N.J.: Revell, 1974.

Solomon, C. *Handbook to happiness.* Wheaton: Tyndale, 1971.

Starbuck, E. *The psychology of religion.* New York: Scribner's, 1901.

Stedman, R. *Body life.* Glendale: Regal, 1972.

Stotland, E. *The psychology of hope: An integration of experimental, clinical and social approaches.* San Francisco: Jossey-Bass, 1969.

Stott, J. *Basic Christianity.* Grand Rapids: Eerdmans, 1971.

Thiessen, H. *Introductory lectures in systematic theology.* Grand Rapids: Eerdmans, 1949.

Thorne, F. Principles of personality counseling. Brandon, Vt.:Journal of Clinical Psychology, 1950.

Tolman, E. C. *Behavior and psychological man: Essays in motivation and learning.* Berkeley: University of California, 1958.

Tournier, P. *The meaning of persons.* New York: Harper and Row, 1957.

Tournier, P. *Guilt and grace.* New York: Harper and Row, 1962.

Tweedie, D. *Logotherapy and the Christian faith.* Grand Rapids: Baker, 1961.

Wagner, M. *Put it all together.* Grand Rapids: Zondervan, 1974.

Wagner, M. *The sensation of being somebody.* Grand Rapids: Zondervan, 1975.

White, A. *A history of the warfare of science with theology in Christendom.* New York: Appleton, 1898.

Wright, N. *Communication: Key to your marriage.* Glendale: Regal, 1974.

REFERENCE NOTES

1. Carlson, D. E. *Jesus' style of relating: The search for a biblical view of counseling.* Paper presented at the Conference on Research in Mental Health and Religious Behavior, Atlanta, January 24-26, 1976.
2. Clement, P. *Behavior modification of the Spirit.* Paper presented at a meeting of the Western Association of Christians for Psychological Studies, Santa Barbara, California, June, 1976.
3. Ellis, A. *The psychotherapist's case against religion.* Paper presented at a meeting of the New York Humanist Society, New York, 1965.
4. Greenson, R. R. *The conflict between religion and psychoanalysis.* Los Angeles: Pacifica Tape Library, n.d.
5. Sutherland, P. and Poelstra, P. *Aspects of integration.* Paper presented at the meeting of the Western Association of Christians for Psychological Studies, Santa Barbara, California, June, 1976.

ANNOTATED BIBLIOGRAPHY

The following annotated list of books and articles is designed for the person interested in pursuing in greater depth specific aspects of the integration of psychology and theology. It is not meant to be exhaustive but rather to survey some of the helpful offerings in the field of integration. These works represent a variety of theological and psychological viewpoints but all either make significant contributions to our understanding of the interrelationships of psychology and theology or represent viewpoints that must be dealt with in any comprehensive integration.

GENERAL PSYCHOLOGY (INTRODUCTORY ISSUES, SURVEYS AND PERSPECTIVES)

Collins, G. *The rebuilding of psychology*. Wheaton: Tyndale, 1977.

This is probably the most helpful survey of basic issues on the integration of psychology and theology currently available. Especially helpful is Collins's nontechnical summary of the underlying presuppositions held by most non-Christian psychologists (empiricism, determinism, naturalism, reductionism) and his evaluation and modification of these assumptions in the light of biblical revelation.

Cosgrove, M. *The essence of human nature*. Grand Rapids: Zondervan, 1977.

A very helpful book that demonstrates the limits of the scientific method in dealing with human nature, especially its nonmaterial aspect. This book is part of the Christian Free University Curriculum, a series of supplementary readings designed for use by undergraduate students who desire to relate their Christian faith to a variety of academic disciplines.

Farnsworth, K. Models for the integration of psychology and theology. *Journal of the American Scientific Affiliation,* 1978, *30,* 6-9.

The author proposes a series of five models on the relationship of psychology and Christianity similar to the four described in this book. The orientation is phenomenological, and the emphasis is on the whole person being involved in integration.

Jeeves, M. *Psychology and Christianity: The view both ways.* Downers Grove, Ill.: InterVarsity, 1976.

An introduction to the encounter between psychology and Christianity written by an experimental psychologist who specializes in the experimental study of thinking and neuropsychology. It contains a good discussion of the presuppositions of psychology and a way of looking at apparent conflicts between psychology and Christianity. Unfortunately (as the title indicates), the book follows a strongly Parallels model. It is a view both ways rather than a true integration.

Meehl, P. (Ed.). *What then is man?* St. Louis: Concordia, 1958.

This is one of the first sophisticated discussions of the relationship of psychology and theology by theologically orthodox authors. It includes discussions on conversion, determinism, guilt, and psychopathology. It is authored by a group of Lutheran theologians and psychologists.

PHILOSOPHY AND THEOLOGY

The writings in this section, while not specifically psychological, provide a great deal of helpful background material for those interested in a serious study of the integration of psychology and theology.

Holmes, A. *All truth is God's truth.* Grand Rapids: Eerdmans, 1977.

This book spells out the basic assumption necessary to the integration of psychology and theology—the belief that all truth is God's truth. A readable and relatively nontechnical presentation and excellent supplementary reading for an initial course in integration.

Laidlaw, J. *The Bible doctrine of man.* Edinburgh: T. & T. Clark, 1879.

This is a high point in the evangelical theological understanding of the human being. There is no work of similar value available today.

Niebuhr, H. R. *Christ and culture.* New York: Harper, 1951.

A survey of five approaches that Christians have historically taken in relating their religious faith to a secular world. It is helpful in setting the problem of the relationship of psychology to theology in the context of the larger problem of relating the secular and the sacred.

Sanderson, W. Christian empiricism as an integrating perspective in psychology and theology. *Christian Scholar's Review,* 1978, *8,* 32-41.

A sophisticated theoretical discussion and argument for a Christian empirical foundation for the integration of psychology and Christianity. This is not for the beginner in the area of integration.

Warfield, B. B. The emotional life of our Lord. In S. G. Craig (Ed.), *The person and work of Christ.* Philadelphia: Presbyterian and Reformed, 1950. (Originally published in *Biblical and theological studies* [New York: Scribner, 1912].)

While the language and style are dated, Warfield gives a full and profound analysis of Christ's emotions. Written over fifty years ago, the work gives a much-needed balance to the notion propounded by many Evangelicals that emotions are second class (or excess baggage) in comparison with cognition.

Wolfe, D. Reflections on Christian empiricism: Thoughts on William Sanderson's proposal. *Christian Scholar's Review,* 1978, *8,* 42-45.

A critique of the theory that Christian empiricism is an adequate foundation for integration. The author shows that empiricism itself is an interpretation of the data rather than being neutral or objective, as Sanderson assumes. Again, this is not for the beginner.

SUBSTANTIVE INTEGRATION AT THE THEOLOGICAL LEVEL

To date most orthodox attempts at relating psychology and theology have suffered from a lack of theological sophistication. They tend to rely on a proof-texting of Scripture or on an isolated use of Scripture. Here are two notable exceptions.

Hulme, W. *Counseling and theology.* Philadelphia: Fortress, 1956.

To our way of thinking, this book contains the most able discussion of the relation of specific theological doctrines to concerns facing the psychologist. This material includes a discussion of the nature of the human being, the concept of sin, the need for confession, the doctrinal basis for counseling, the Atonement, sanctification, and grace. It should be read by every pastor and theologian interested in counseling as well as by every student of psychology desiring to integrate the biblical and psychological realms.

Hulme, W. *The dynamics of sanctification.* Minneapolis: Augsburg, 1966.

An excellent discussion of the doctrine of sanctification, especially in terms of its implications for personal and spiritual growth. The chapter entitled "Sin—Weakness or Defiance" grapples well with the issue of responsibility. This work also contains a good discussion of forgiveness and justification.

CHRISTIAN PERSONALITY THEORY

The books in this section were written primarily for the lay person. They contain a variety of helpful insights, and at the same time they all make significant contributions to the integration of psychology and theology.

Darling, H. *Man in triumph.* Grand Rapids: Zondervan, 1969.

A thorough review (though varying in quality) of the various personality theories from a Christian point of view. In the final chapter Darling suggests an integrated model of the Christian life.

Hodge, M. *Your fear of love.* Garden City, N.Y.: Doubleday, 1967.

A sensitive discussion from a loosely Rogerian framework of all of the factors in interpersonal relations that make individuals feel vulnerable—love, sex, anger, and intimacy. This volume provides helpful information on human emotions, but it is weak theologically at points.

Kamm, A. van. *Religion and personality.* New York: Doubleday, Image Books, 1968.

A superior discussion by a Catholic priest of the importance and place of religion (Evangelicals should read "God and Christian experience") in a believer's life and personality. It is written from an existential perspective.

Narramore, B. *You're someone special.* Grand Rapids: Zondervan, 1978.

An integrative discussion of self-love and self-esteem. Special attention is given to the following: the biblical basis for a balanced self-esteem; the relation of pride and humility to self-esteem; and the early determinants of self-esteem.

Tournier, P. *The meaning of persons.* New York: Harper and Row, 1957.

An excellent discussion of the uniqueness of the human being and the importance of meaningful interpersonal experiences in a frequently impersonal world. Special attention is given to the role of the doctor-patient relationship in the healing process.

Wagner, M. *Put it all together.* Grand Rapids: Zondervan, 1974.

An excellent integrative discussion of three negative emotions: fear, guilt, and hostility. Trained in theology and psychology, the author wrestles with integration and brings his wide knowledge of Scripture to bear on these frequently devastating emotions.

Wagner, M. *The sensation of being somebody.* Grand Rapids: Zondervan, 1975.

This is a sequel to the previous volume. It has an excellent integrative discussion of the self-concept, and it brings the same wide understanding to such specific topics as the need for security, belongingness, worth, and competence. Especially helpful is his discussion of the role of our relationship with each member of the Trinity in developing a positive self-concept.

GUILT AND CONSCIENCE

Narramore, B. Guilt: Where theology and psychology meet. *Journal of Psychology and Theology,* 1974, 2, 18-25.

This is the first in a series of four articles that discuss the central role of guilt in psychopathology and the integration of guilt into a psychodynamic perspective.

Pattison, M. Ego morality: An emerging psychotherapeutic concept. *Psychoanalytic Review,* 1968, 55, 187-222.

An excellent discussion of ego and superego morality (from a psychoanalytic perspective), with clear distinctions drawn between the destructive, primitive guilt of superego morality and the constructive, existential guilt of an adult ego morality. It also contains a stimulating discussion of forgiveness and the role of the therapist's values in the therapeutic process.

Stein, E. *Guilt: Theory and therapy.* Philadelphia: Westminster, 1969.

Each of the first four chapters presents a very clear, concise summary of a major theory of the development of guilt (Sigmund Freud, Melanie Klein, Eric Fromm, and David Ausubel). Although heavily influenced by the theology of Tillich, Stein's later chapters nevertheless shed a good deal of light on the contributions of theology to our understanding of the problem of guilt.

Thielicke, H. *Theological ethics.* Edited by William H. Lazareth. 2 vols. Philadelphia: Fortress, 1966.

Chapter 15, "The Evangelical View of Conscience," is a most penetrating theological analysis of conscience; Thielicke discusses the sources of unrest of conscience in both the redeemed and nonredeemed, the nature of attempts to pacify one's own conscience, and the implications of justification and sanctification for the functioning of conscience.

Tournier, P. *Guilt and grace.* New York: Harper and Row, 1962.

This is Tournier's most conceptual book. He discusses various aspects of guilt: its subtle manifestations; its destructiveness; true and false guilt; and the relation of the Atonement and unconditional love to guilt feelings. It has helpful theoretical and practical insights.

PASTORAL COUNSELING

Adams, J. *Competent to counsel.* Grand Rapids: Baker, 1970.

This is Adams's first volume in the area of counseling and his most polemic book. He severely criticizes the presuppositions at work in most existing approaches to counseling, and argues for "nouthetic" counseling—a very directive form of counsel. This book has been favorably received in some circles; however, it tends (in the steps of Mowrer) toward an external, behavioral focus on sins rather than sin and is weak on the role of on-going, intimate relationships in the growth process.

Adams, J. *The Christian counselor's manual.* Grand Rapids: Baker, 1973.

A development and application of the theoretical position propounded in *Competent to counsel.*

Clinebell, H. *Basic types of pastoral counseling.* Nashville: Abingdon, 1966.

This is perhaps the most helpful book available on pastoral counseling. Although it is not written from a distinctively evangelical perspective, it presents in a clear style a realistic model of pastoral counseling that attempts neither to duplicate professional psychotherapy nor to provide a Band-Aid approach. It emphasizes the pastoral counselor's role in the following aspects of counseling: using supportive counseling methods; improving counselees' interpersonal relationships in order to develop their strengths; helping the counselee to cope with the present and plan for the future;

134 ■ INTEGRATION OF PSYCHOLOGY AND THEOLOGY

helping the counselee to confront the realities of life; and dealing with what Clinebell calls "the vertical dimension."

Crabb, L. *Effective biblical counseling.* Grand Rapids: Zondervan, 1977.

This is an expansion of his earlier book, Basic principles of biblical counseling *(1975). The approach is primarily directive, rational-emotive counseling, and this is integrated with many scriptural insights.*

Hulme, W. *Pastoral care come of age.* Nashville: Abingdon, 1970.

A helpful historical survey of pastoral care, with suggestions concerning its role in the ministry of the church and discussion of specific issues such as guilt, responsibility, and ministry in situations involving death.

Narramore, C. *The psychology of counseling.* Grand Rapids: Zondervan, 1960.

A good introduction to counseling for pastors and other Christian workers. It contains succinct statements of what are essentially nondirective principles of counseling and some practical suggestions.

MATURITY

Carter, J. Maturity: Psychological and biblical. *Journal of Psychology and Theology,* 1974, 2, 89-96.

An analysis of five dimensions that can be used to compare Christian maturity and psychological maturity (a realistic view of self and others; accepting oneself and others; living in the present with long-term goals; having values; and using one's ability and interest in the task of daily living). These dimensions are illustrated by means of secular psychological concepts and Scripture passages.

Carter, J. Personality and Christian maturity: A process congruity model. *Journal of Psychology and Theology,* 1974, 2, 190-201.

An integrated model of Christian maturity and personality built on the personality theories of Gendlin, Jung, and Rogers and the biblical concepts of renewal (actualization) of the image of God and the wholeness of the human being.

Climes, M. Sin and maturity. *Journal of Psychology and Theology,* 1977, 5, 183-196.

A challenging analysis of what is and what is not sin and how these are involved in Christian maturity. It is written by a biblical theologian.

Oakland, J. Self-actualization and sanctification. *Journal of Psychology and Theology,* 1974, 2, 202-209.

A thoughtful integrative model of the relationship between sanctification and Maslow's concept of self-actualization.

Oakland, J. The introjected and the intrinsic in psychology and Christianity. *Journal of Psychology and Theology,* 1977, 5, 91-94.

An analysis of the relationship of extrinsic (introjected) and intrinsic Christian experience to Christian maturity.

RELIGION AND PSYCHOLOGY (NON-EVANGELICAL)

Daim, W. *Depth psychology and salvation.* New York: Unger, 1963.

Daim, a European and a Catholic existential analyst, describes how various objects (nonabsolutes) are substituted for the one absolute (God) and how to find God therapeutically. This is difficult reading for the beginner.

Homan, P. (Ed.). *The dialogue between theology and psychology.* Chicago: University of Chicago Press, 1968.

A mixed group of readings given by graduates of the University of Chicago's psychology and religion program. Chapters 1, 3, 4, and 5 make the book worthwhile.

Oden, T. *Kerygma and counseling.* Philadelphia: Westminster, 1966.

An outstanding attempt at the integration of a loose Rogerian perspective and a conservative neoorthodox Christianity. The comprehensive model of a Christian integrated therapy outlined in chapter 2 is by itself worth the price of the book.

SECULAR PSYCHOLOGY

A number of secular writers have produced works with significant implications for the integration of psychology and theology. The following books are listed, not necessarily because we find the viewpoint consistent with biblical revelation, but because they represent definitive points of view that need to be considered in effecting an in-depth integration of psychology and Christianity.

Brenner, C. *An elementary textbook of psychoanalysis.* New York: Doubleday, Anchor Books, 1957.

Freud's voluminous writings make it nearly impossible for nonspecialists to gain an appreciation of the fundamentals of his thought. Brenner's book is an excellent survey of the major tenets of psychoanalysis. It is especially useful for those wanting more than a superficial secondary presentation of psychoanalytic thinking.

Freud, S. [*Future of an illusion.*] In A. Strackey (trans.), *The complete psychological works of Sigmund Freud.* Vol. 21, pp. 5-56. London: Hogarth, 1961. (Originally published, 1927).

This is Freud's discussion of the origin of belief in God. Next to his emphasis on sexual matters, this is the aspect of his theory most frequently criticized by Christians; and for this reason, it deserves to be read.

Glasser, W. *Reality therapy.* New York: Harper and Row, 1965.

An exposition of a primarily directive therapeutic modality emphasizing responsibility for one's actions and awareness of the consequences of maladaptive behavior. It minimizes the influence of the past, and for this reason and for its emphasis on behavioral responsibility it has been well received in many Christian circles. The behavioral focus and the works (legalistic) orientation ("If people will act right, they will feel right.") raise serious theological and therapeutic issues, however.

Horney, K. *Neurosis and human growth.* New York: Norton, 1937.

A penetrating analysis of the origins of neurosis. Her discussion of the "search for glory" (the child's quest to fulfill feelings of omnipotence) as the root of neurotic functioning has striking parallels to the biblical concept of sin as the rejection of creatureliness and the desire to be God-like. This is highly stimulating reading for those interested in integration.

Mowrer, O. H. *The crisis in psychiatry and religion.* Princeton, N.J.: Van Nostrand, 1961.

A collection of essays highly critical of Freudian psychoanalysis and its concept of psychological "sickness" (which is viewed as Freudian irresponsibility). It contains a much-needed emphasis on personal responsibility, morality, and honesty; and it is of interest to the Christian because Mowrer was influential in the development of Jay Adams's thinking and his development of nouthetic counseling. Mowrer tends, however, to misrepresent psychoanalysis. Theologically, although he speaks of sin, it is not the Judeo-Christian view of an offense against God; he also rejects the concept of vicarious atonement.

Rogers, C. *On becoming a person.* Boston: Houghton-Mifflin, 1961.

An excellent summary of Rogers's understanding of the nature of the human being, education, counseling, and growth. The chapter entitled "This Is Me" gives deep insight into the development of his theoretical viewpoint. It traces his life from boyhood in a conservative Protestant family, through college and seminary studies, to his work as a professional psychologist. His shifting views on the nature of the human being is especially significant in light of his later belief in the essential goodness of the human race.

Skinner, B. F. *Beyond freedom and dignity.* New York: Knopf, 1971.

Every student of psychology should read Skinner's attack on the concept of human freedom. The implications of this philosophical perspective for issues such as responsibility and human dignity must be grappled with in any effective integration.

INDEX